Ghosts
of the NHS

Ghosts

of the NHS

and Other Spirits I Have Known

GLYNIS AMY ALLEN

Glynis Amy Allen © 2020

All rights reserved in accordance with the Copyright,
Designs and Patents Act 1988.

No parts of this publication may be reproduced, stored in a
retrieval system, or transmitted in any form or by any means
whatsoever without the prior permission of the publisher.

A record of this publication is available from the British Library.

ISBN 978-1-910027-34-9

Typesetting by Wordzworth Ltd
www.wordzworth.com

Cover design by Titanium Design Ltd
www.titaniumdesign.co.uk

Cover image by Adobe Stock
(Licence ADB085734051UK)

Published by Local Legend
www.local-legend.co.uk

This book is dedicated to all the people
who have given me the privilege of telling their stories
and allowing me to bring their spiritual loved ones forward.

Acknowledgements

I am most grateful to all my family, especially Grandma Mac, to my teacher Wendy and to my publisher Nigel Peace.

Disclaimer

www.local-legend.co.uk

About the Author

"I have been blessed," says Glynis, "with amazing spiritual gifts, especially clairvoyance, passed down to me by my Grandma Mac. She would speak to spirits and angels when she needed help, and told me, 'I call them forward, tell them my troubles and ask for their help – they always answer me.' It has been natural – and a privilege – for me to carry on my grandma's work."

This book tells the story of Glynis Allen's spiritual life, especially while working as a senior hospital nurse in the National Health Service for thirty years. You will read true accounts of the ghosts and spirits she encountered, such as seeing the soul leaving the body of the deceased and meeting the guardian spirits of those who were suffering. She was often able to pass on comforting evidence of survival.

Her nursing career was cut short by injury and illness. At the time, this seemed devastating, but Spirit simply had other plans for Glynis! She found that she could know people by their auras and she gained a closer relationship with her spirit guide as she studied to develop her mediumship.

"Now," she says, "I spend my life guiding others with their lives' challenges."

"It is rare," writes the publisher, "to find an account of mediumship and communication with the spirit world that is told in such a down-to-earth way. Glynis gives us one extraordinary story after another, yet with detailed authenticity, humour and genuine compassion. This is a remarkable book, the truth of which is very hard to deny."

Contents

The Staff Nurse said, "I'm just going to fetch some towels so you carry on washing the patient down."

I was cleaning the patient's fingernails when I thought I could smell white lilies. Not only that, I definitely felt a presence. When I lifted my head up I saw, on the other side of the bed, a nurse with a big Red Cross on her pinafore. She just stood there, as real as anything, as though I could reach out and touch her. She looked radiant. My hands started to tingle, like pins and needles.

I thought to myself, 'No-one has come into the cubicle, so who is this nurse?'

The Staff Nurse came back soon after and said, "Oh, she's been here, then."

"Who is she?" I asked, a little nervously.

"Oh, it's the Grey Lady. She always comes when patients are ready to pass over."

1

Who Am I?

I was born in the snowstorm of 1947! My Grandma Mac delivered me – she was known as the local Wise Woman and everyone came to see her for advice. She held me in her arms and said to my mother, "You have a gifted child here, Mary, and she will bring happiness to many people."

Her reason for saying that was because I was born with 'the caul' over my face and the old wives' tale is that such a child is a Caulbearer, one who will have second sight. The caul is a piece of membrane that covers the new-born's head but only very rarely, about one in eighty thousand births. Some people refer to it as being 'born behind the veil' and Caulbearer children are often regarded as strange by other people because we have unusual perception, perhaps a sense of knowing something before it happens. That was certainly me as a child. I would also see colours around people, quite unaware then that these are called auras.

My first encounter with Spirit was when my Grandad died. We were a Catholic family and it was the custom to keep the deceased in the house until their burial. He was laid in his coffin in a bedroom with the curtains closed and candles burning at the side of the room. For an eleven year old child, it was rather scary. I sat sewing downstairs with my Grandma when she turned to me and said, "You need to see your Grandad."

As I walked into the bedroom there was a mist floating above Grandad in his coffin and I could see a silver cord reaching up towards the ceiling. Grandma said, "Kiss Grandad goodbye." As I bent down to kiss him I heard his voice clearly saying in my mind, "Look after your Mam."

I turned to Grandma and told her what I'd seen and heard. Straight away I could feel she was going to tell me something important because she was a very straight talker and she had her serious face on.

"I never told you this before," she said, "but you have an amazing gift – you can talk with spirits. I can also connect with Spirit but Grandad forbade me to do so because of our Catholic faith. You must use your gift wisely, although I must also warn you not to tell people you can see these things. You might be taken away and locked up because folk say you're mad."

I asked her why was there a silver cord hanging down below the ceiling and she told me that we all have a cord attached to us from the Heavens, and this breaks when we die. "Not everyone can see this," she said, "and it proves to me that you are one of God's helpers."

Feeling a little bolder, I asked her why people brought their cups with tea leaves in them to her, and then sometimes cry. "How did you know about that?" she said. I told her that I'd seen her and Peggie through the window looking into Peggie's cup; Grandma was shaking her head and Peggie was crying.

"You don't miss much, you sharp beggar," she said. "Let's just forget about it for a while." As Grandma was talking to me, her aura changed from green/blue to a wonderful purple edged with yellow. I loved her so much.

For a while I found myself thinking back to what Grandad had said, "Look after your Mam." She didn't look ill, she wasn't complaining about anything and she was still going out with her friends. But a few days later my father left her for another woman. Mam took it very badly, she wouldn't get out of bed or wash and she lost weight. The doctor wanted her to go into a psychiatric hospital to recover from the breakdown but she refused. "My daughter and Mam will look after me."

I then realised why Grandad had said what he did – he must have known that father was leaving us. Mam was devastated but I wasn't, in fact I was glad he had gone because he was an alcoholic and physically abusive to me and Mam when he had the drink inside him. He was a womaniser, too, and a thief: he would take money out of Mam's purse and he even sold a watch I had for Christmas, said I'd lost it and gave me a good hiding. Then a girl at school was showing everyone her new watch – it was mine, he had sold it for a couple of pints of beer. He also sold the free coal we had so we were left cold with no fire.

So there was just me and my mother now but we were okay with Grandma's help. I stayed off school to help look after Mam.

One day there came a knock on the door. It was Gypsy Rose Lee, a friend of my mother's, who lived in the wood across from our house. "Mam is poorly," I said, feeling very grown up, "and she doesn't want to see anyone." "Out of the way, girl, she will see me," she said, pushing me to one side. Then she said, "Make two cups of tea and go out to play. Then come and see me in my caravan later." I was very annoyed!

When I saw her leave I couldn't get back into the house quick enough to make sure Mam was okay. I picked up the teacups to wash them, being very careful because my mother had a nice china cup with roses on it. But I was shocked when I looked into it because I could see numbers, images and figures. I understood then what my Grandma had said about a gift. I could see things that no-one else could, things that explained what was going to happen, and I felt a power surge in my body with my hands starting to tingle. So, I had the same gift as my Grandma, I could read tea leaves. What a revelation.

From that day on, I looked into everyone's cup. In my mother's I had seen a pharaoh's head, a coffin with the letter J, a man kneeling in the rain, a man in bed, the letters JM, a pram with two babies in it and a nurse. It was all so vivid that I wrote it down and kept the paper. Years later, I looked at it again and this is what had happened:

Pharaoh's head – my Uncle Derek was called up for his national service and sent to Egypt.
A coffin with the letter J – my Grandpa Johnny passed away very suddenly.
A man kneeling in the rain – my father had a pit accident, with rocks 'raining down' on him.
A man in bed – my father was then in hospital. (Mam visited him even though they were separated.)
The letters JM – my father Jack and mother Mary were reunited after the accident.
A pram with two babies in it – my two younger sisters, Denise and Janet.
The nurse – well, that's me!

I'd had no ambition to be a nurse, it was just fate how it came about. I wanted to follow my mother into the Women's Royal Air Force to be a mechanic like her, or perhaps work in a circus as an acrobat. I was a very fit child and loved P.E. at school. My friend Irene and I used to practise acrobatics, training for work in the circus next time it came to our village, and she would swing me around by the legs.

I would also run every day and was soon running for local clubs; my mother had also been an athlete and had won cups, but sadly I never did. My uncle encouraged me and bought me some spiked running shoes so I used to train with him and his stopwatch every evening. One day, when I came to put my spiked shoes on they had disappeared. I asked my father if he'd seen them and he told me that he'd sold them. Then he said, "Go and make your potions with her next door, you pair of witches." With that he shoved me into the coalhouse, locked the door and left me there for two hours while he went to the pub. He had a grey and red aura, not a good combination.

Mam had a friend who worked in a wool mill at Home Firth and the next thing I knew I was starting work, catching a bus at 5.30 a.m. because it took an hour and half to get there. My friend Jenny also started work there the same day and we were trained to spin and get the knots out of the wool. One cold, snowy day we decided to have our lunch sandwiches in the lower floor where the wool was stored. We were chatting about girly things when someone walked past us in a white frilly cap and a black dress; we heard the rustling of keys and noticed the scent of lily of the valley. She turned to look at us... and vanished. We got up and ran!

Later we learned that this was the spirit of the mill owner's sister, who had fallen down a flight of stairs there and died. She was known to be wicked, only giving the working children bread and water and even locking them in the mill overnight to finish off an order. She certainly had an evil look in her eye. Not surprisingly, we left soon after that.

By the time I was seventeen I was looking after my younger sisters as well as going to work and looking after Mam, so I didn't go out much. The birth of my sisters had changed my life dramatically and any free time I had was caring for them, because by now Mam had turned to alcohol to help her cope with life. We lived next door to my grandparents so at least I had them for support. But my Grandma Mac was growing frail and needed help with bathing so that became my job too; there wasn't any social care then as there is now, although saying that she would never have accepted it. She was a staunch Catholic lady. Every Friday, Father Regan would be seen cycling around the village on his old bike and he'd call in for his half-crown and a chat with Grandad. I loved those tales of when they were both lads in Ireland.

But I felt I was growing old before my time, because of all these chores. When I did have some time to myself I would read over and over again a Ladybird book my Grandma had bought me about Joan of Arc. I loved her story, especially how Archangel Gabriel had come to her and said she would lead an army into battle to save France. I loved her because she heard voices and saw visions – just like me.

Grandma Mac grew herbs and she taught me many things about nature and using herbs for healing. One time, I ripped my knee open when climbing on a hut; it was a very deep cut and probably should have had stitches in it. But she applied a bread poultice smeared with nettle and lettuce leaves, leaving it on for three days. When the dressing came off, the wound was healed. People would come from miles around for her healing potions. She would send me to look in people's dustbins for glass jars, which she cleaned with washing powder and then put in the oven to sterilise. I learned from her and now also grow herbs and make healing potions.

"It's about time," she said to me one day, "you started going out and enjoying yourself. You don't want to end up an old spinster with no children to look after you in your old age."

So when my friend May asked me to go to a dance with her, I agreed, and Grandma promised to look after Mam and the kids. I soaked a net underskirt in sugar to make it stiff and wore some patent black stilettos. I felt like the belle of the ball. We were dancing together when, as I twirled around, I saw a very handsome young man looking my way.

"See that man over there with the green eyes," I said to May. "I'm going to marry him." She just laughed and said, "You don't even know him." But I knew he was my soulmate, the way I knew so many other things. He asked me out and more than fifty years later the rest is history.

I was born with the ability to communicate with Spirit and I believe that we all are. But a lot of people do not embrace this gift, and even fear it, because it's hard to understand. However, it's my experience that once we open up to the spirit world and start communicating with them, our lives will become more fulfilled.

Firstly, let's be clear about the difference between ghosts and spirits! A ghost is the soul of a deceased person: they may appear fully clothed and look just like a real person but they often seem vague and hazy, not interacting with us. They once lived on Earth yet, for whatever reason, they are still holding on to places that were familiar to them and have not 'gone to the light'. So ghosts are spirit, but not all spirits are ghosts. For the great majority of people, their spirit leaves the body on death when the silver cord is broken. Spirits have full consciousness on the other side of life, keeping their memories of physical existence, and they are always around us.

I also learned very early on that there's a difference between a psychic and a medium. It is a little complicated because not all mediums are psychic and not all psychics are mediums. A psychic will use their intuition to receive information about someone and often will use tools such as cards or runes as a divination tool. Regrettably, there are a number of fake psychics around who are being fraudulent and earning money from unfortunate, grieving people who need to have contact with loved ones who have passed on. It hurts my heart greatly that people can be so cruel. Fake psychics will often use a method called 'cold reading' and I myself was the victim of this many years ago when I went to a Psychic Fair, where this man gave me the impression that he could contact my Grandma Mac. Now, I would like to meet anyone who could get one over on my grandma!

"I have an old lady here with grey hair," he said. Hmm, great start. "And there's a man who passed with a heart condition and who suffered breathing problems." Well, anyone with a heart problem will also have breathing problems, and we all know that heart disease is the most common killer. "This lady is very proud of you," he went on, "and the way you have brought up your family. You have one child and one in spirit which you lost, but hadn't realised you were pregnant—"

I'd heard enough. Everything he had said was rubbish and he had the cheek to charge me forty pounds. He quickly got up, collected his things and left.

On the other hand, a genuine medium connects with a person's loved ones in spirit and passes on messages from them – it's communication with the dead, and a medium usually has a spirit guide who helps to bring loved ones forward.

For the record, I am both – a psychic medium! I have all the 'clair' gifts, with clairvoyance and clairaudience being the strongest. Clairvoyance (meaning 'clear vision' in French) is the ability to perceive things without using the five normal human senses. It is a knowing about someone or something, seeing the past, present and future. Sometimes, clairvoyants can actually see and interact with spirit people: I can see what the spirit was wearing when they passed over or they might show me a familiar object or describe what someone had put in their coffin. When I relay these facts to a client it is proof that, yes, Spirit is here with us while we do the reading.

When a spirit speaks to me, I hear it clearly in my head and this is called clairaudience; on occasion, a word may be shouted out from nowhere. Once I was giving a reading for a man who had lost his wife and the words "He betrayed me" were shouted out. The man immediately recognised his wife's voice and fainted; when he came to, he left the room fast.

Quite similar to clairvoyance, though without the direct spirit contact, are clairsentience and claircognisance. These are difficult to describe, just an ability to know when something is right or wrong. For example, one day I was walking in the woods with my dogs and my daughter when I had a strong feeling of danger; I knew that something bad might happen if we carried on that pathway through the woods. "Let's walk the other way, I feel unsafe," I said and my daughter agreed that she felt it too. Later we learned that a woman and her dog had been attacked by two men with three Staffordshire terriers, and the little dog had to be put to sleep.

Clairsentience can also involve a physical feeling. When I give a reading, I may get a chest pain or a violent headache or even a severe shortness of breath. The spirit person communicating is telling me about their condition before they died.

The last of the 'clairs', one that is quite rare, is clairgustience meaning an ability to taste or smell something evidential. It could be something mundane associated with the spirit that identifies them, like a love for cherry pie! Once I was doing a reading for a lady who had lost her Mum and I could smell Evening in Paris which was a very old perfume, popular back in the Fifties. The client said, "My Mum is here, she always used that perfume." Her mother replied, "You still have my bottle of perfume" – proof that her spirit was there with us.

Now, I don't always get everything right. But I never lie to make myself look good and if I cannot make a connection with Spirit then I say so and make no charge. We will never be able to absolutely prove or disprove what happens after we die, but so many correct messages add up to strong evidence.

Both ghosts and spirits are around me all the time – I see them and I hear them. Judge for yourself as you read my stories…

2

Professional Nursing

I left home and got married at eighteen. At first, we lived with my mother-in-law who was on her own and it was working well until she had an operation that went wrong and could not go back to work. So I decided to get a job, Flora would look after our kids and I would pay her. She was a truly amazing lady.

It was as though 'someone' was guiding me at the Job Centre. The first post I saw advertised was for a Nursing Auxiliary at Oakwood Hall Hospital; I went straight there for an interview and I got the job. But when I walked onto the ward on my first day, I was scared: it had a feeling of sorrow and a distinct scent of white lilies. I had only ever seen one dead person, my Grandad, and I was dreading seeing someone die and then having to do the last offices for them. Still, my colleagues were amazing and taught me so much, even if they did play pranks on me. One day the Ward Sister said, "Glynis, would you go to cubicle three for a long stand, please?" Of course, I couldn't find a stand when I went there... but I took it all in good humour and soon fitted in happily.

After a while, they guided me through doing the last offices for a lady. It was a privilege to do this but, for me, it was sometimes scary because the deceased person would actually speak to me! Usually this was to request that they be buried in something special, such as their wedding dress or a uniform; but I couldn't very well tell the relatives that.

It was only my second deceased patient that brought my first encounter with the ghostly Grey Lady. The Staff Nurse said she was just going to fetch some towels and asked me to carry on washing the patient. I was concentrating on cleaning the finger-nails when I smelled white lilies… but not only that, I could feel a presence nearby. When I lifted my head up I saw, on the other side of the bed, a nurse standing there with a large Red Cross on her pinafore; she seemed real and solid and radiant, not a ghostly apparition, as though I could reach out and touch her. My hands started to tingle with pins and needles (I came to learn that this is one of the signs to notice in these moments.) No-one had come into the cubicle so who was this nurse? The Staff Nurse came back and said casually, "Oh, she has been here, then. It's the Grey Lady – she often comes when patients are moribund and ready to pass over. Yes, she leaves the scent of white lilies." I had been standing there with a ghost, just one of many such encounters I would have.

Things took a turn for the worse soon after this, when I started bleeding heavily. I was making a bed when my colleague commented that I looked really pale and at that very moment I heard my Grandma's voice saying, "Cancer!" I was sent home to see my doctor who referred me to see a consultant the next day; he checked me out with a colposcope and said I needed a radical hysterectomy as soon as possible because I had cervical cancer.

As I lay on the operating table, I could feel the last two stitches being put into my abdomen and then I saw a vision – a radiant face smiling down at me. She had blonde curls and I thought, 'Why isn't she wearing a theatre hat and gown?' Still, I assumed she was one of the operating theatre staff. I heard the surgeon say, "She's coming round, give her more anaesthetic." It was Friday the 13th and I was having an operation to save my life. If my Grandma had not made herself known and spoken to me, I would have been dead.

Later, I could still see that face in my mind so I made an excuse to visit the theatre, taking the staff some biscuits, and asked who the nurse with the curly blonde hair was. They told me there was no-one like that in any of the theatres so now I was convinced that it had been an angel come to reassure me.

I went back to work after three months and the Ward Sister told me she had referred me to do professional nurse training. I was astonished because I had no qualifications, I'd had to leave school to look after my sisters while my mother was ill in hospital. But Sister said, "Once in a while, someone stands out to me and that's you. My only wish is that you come back to us when you are qualified." So once again my path was being guided. I could not believe I was going to be a qualified nurse, but then I thought back to that tea leaf reading many years ago… The nurse was me.

My colleagues taught me a lot back then, even with their pranks, for example how to handle doctors who thought nurses were beneath them. One such doctor was quite elderly and had nine children to support, so he would go into the kitchen when we were giving out meals and steal the cheese and biscuits and cakes, anything he could get his hands on. He spoke to us like dirt too so we planned to catch him out. Someone brought in a pen with invisible ink that turned your hands purple if you touched it and we wrapped up cakes, cheese, biscuits and packets of soup and drew a cross on them. He stole the lot and came in next day with bandaged hands, pretending that he'd hurt them burning rubbish in the garden. Soon he announced that he was taking six weeks off to go abroad, but he never came back. Later he sent us a postcard saying, "Sorry for pinching the food. I am so ashamed you caught me out."

My psychic senses saved me again one night when I was driving home after my last shift in my beloved grey Ford Escort car; it was ten o'clock and very cold and foggy. I usually gave someone a lift home but on this particular night I was alone, driving very slowly because the visibility was so bad and with the radio switched off so I could concentrate on the road. As I came to a dip in the road, the back seat started to squeak as though someone was jumping up and down on it; the noise got louder and I was worried that the car was going to break down miles from home. Then I looked in the mirror and saw a man's face looking back at me! No-one could have got into my car because the keys had been locked away at work.

"Who are you?" I asked, as calmly as I could and heard a voice whisper, "Danger!" in reply.

Well, I got home but didn't say anything because no-one would have believed me. On instinct, though, I took the car to a local garage the following day for testing. Later, the garage owner phoned me to say that the car was really dangerous: it was actually two different cars welded together. He remembered the car, or rather half of it – a man had crashed it and died, and this garage owner had towed it in himself. I was totally shocked. Had I not decided to check the car, or had taken it to a different garage, I would never have known. But the spirit on the back seat had warned me and I often wonder just who that was – perhaps the man who had crashed the car?

One Monday afternoon I went in for a late shift and the first task to greet me was to lay out a lady who had died and do the last offices for her. By now, doing this last thing for a patient didn't worry me. This particular patient had died with liver cancer and had only been with us for a few hours, so we had no notes or the results of any investigations yet. I set up my trolley with everything I needed, put on a gown and double gloves because she looked so yellow that I wanted to make sure I was protected from whatever she might have suffered from. It took me a while to do the work as I had to keep washing her.

That done, I carried on with my usual work but felt a bit nauseated and didn't have anything to eat. I was glad when the time came to go home but, the following day, I felt poorly and saw in the mirror that my eyes looked a bit yellow. The doctor was called and I was sent straight to hospital with a suspected liver virus, kept in a cubicle because they thought I might have Hepatitis C. I was barrier nursed for a couple of days until I got the all-clear, with only my husband and mother-in-law allowed to see me.

Around four a.m. I awoke with a jolt. It felt like a cold breeze blowing around me and I shot up in bed, looked around and saw my father standing by a corner of the bed. "Have you died?" I asked him. He just nodded his head, said, "Sorry", and disappeared. I went back to sleep. In the morning, the Ward Sister came in and told me that my father had died during the night. I thanked her for letting me know but I wasn't going to tell her that he had come himself to see me. I was allowed out to go and see my mother for a couple of hours and as I walked into her house the smell of whisky took me aback; she had drunk half a bottle. My two sisters were with her so after a while I said I had to go back to hospital and asked them to let me know when the funeral was.

On the day of his funeral, I was back at home but still very unwell. At the back of the crematorium was the woman my father had left my mother for. Mam was intoxicated again. Afterwards I told her I would not be coming to the wake because I was feeling poorly.

That evening, my uncle telephoned to ask how I was and I told him I'd left because I would only have ended up arguing with my Mam, she being drunk. Then he said, "There's something you ought to know – he was not your real father." I had suspected that already because I'd found both my parents' blood donor cards: I am O Rhesus Negative whilst they were both A Positive. My uncle just confirmed it. He also told me that she'd said she only has two daughters, not three. Well, it wasn't really a surprise to me because I knew I was different and Mam could never get used to it; we had lost any special mother-daughter bond many years ago.

When I was well enough, I went to see her and mentioned that I'd seen my father's 'other woman' at the funeral. She replied, "She should have kept him instead of him coming back to me." At that moment, a cup rolled off the table.

On my last day before setting off for my professional training, a porter came and asked me to help him with a patient in the mortuary. But when I walked in, the door banged shut behind me and I was locked inside. I tried turning the handles but nothing moved. The body of a man was laid out on a slab – we had no fridges back then so patients were taken to another hospital – and I looked at his open eyes, wondering how to get away… I was there for about thirty minutes until the door flew open and an undertaker came in, screaming when he saw me. I told him I'd been locked in but he said the door wasn't locked, giving me a strange look as he stepped aside for me to pass. When I returned to the ward, all the staff were laughing at their trick and waiting to give me a good send-off.

"Why have you been so long? Talking to dead people again?" someone said.

"Yes," I said, "I had a good conservation with the old man on the slab about his journey up to Heaven!"

I started my State Enrolled Nurse training for two years at Fairfields and Moorgate Hospital, sitting in a classroom with twenty-eight other girls. They all looked so young except one, Vera, who was to be my mate throughout our training (until she sadly passed away). We did weeks of theory and none of us knew what to expect when we got onto the wards.

Our first ward was for elderly women, on night duty. Vera was cocky, loud and mischievous, and she loved a cigarette. I told her they would kill her one day but she just laughed and said they kept her sane, having to see so many dead bodies. I would read tea leaves for the staff while Vera kept watch for Matron, then Vera popped out for her ciggie while I watched the patients.

Vera knew that I saw spirits and it never bothered her although it was quite daunting to be on a ward where a lot of patients died. They would give me messages to pass on, like "The money is in the toilet roll holder" or "I don't want our so-and-so to have my clothes"; one old lady said to me, "I know he has been carrying on with her next door, I've seen them in coal shed."

One night, about 3 o'clock, it was cold and windy with the windows rattling and doors banging. I was writing a report when Vera interrupted me with, "Mrs Green is walking up the ward." I retorted that the lady couldn't walk; in any case, I had checked her five minutes before, she was dying and a relative was sitting with her. We both went over to Mrs Green's bed; she had passed over and her son, sat next to her, hadn't noticed.

"Oh my God," said Vera, "I've seen my first ghost. Got to go for a ciggie."

The following night we both saw another ghost in Victorian dress walking down the ward, making a wheezing sound as she came towards us with a whip in her hand. Vera hid in the office while I just stood there and said, "Hello, can I help you?" She then vanished. The hospital had once been a workhouse so we thought she may be connected to that.

We also regularly saw orbs flashing about the ward, some with faces in them, some coloured like bubbles. The first time it happened, Vera looked at me and said, "We are going friggin' crazy in here!" I reassured her that orbs couldn't hurt us; actually, I didn't really know what they were but felt sure they were harmless. Another time, we were together changing a bed when we both saw a figure sitting on a chair in the ward; it had no eyes and the head was just a skull. Vera screamed and ran outside, saying that she was never coming back for anything, but I persuaded her to come back because I couldn't do the work on my own. When we returned, the skull had vanished although it left a putrid smell like rotten vegetables behind. We were glad to leave that ward eventually and we did hear later that nurses often refused to work there because of the ghosts.

I moved on to a Men's Medical Ward where the Charge Nurse was strict. On the first day, I sat in the office with him and saw a spirit man standing beside him in a blue and white striped shirt. The figure said, "This is my son and I am very proud of him. He took no notice of me when I said nursing was for girls." The Charge Nurse thought I was ignoring him and shouted at me to pay attention – I didn't dare say that his Dad was there at his side. But I worked hard on that ward and, when my last day came, I had another meeting with him where he offered me a job on his ward. I replied that, sorry, I had other plans but plucked up the courage to add, "By the way, your Dad is really proud of you." I told him what his Dad had said to me and what he was wearing, and he replied, "Yes, he was buried in his favourite pin-striped blue and white shirt." I went on to say that his Dad thanks him for putting some Brut aftershave on him and that he often followed his son around the ward, so when he could smell Brut he would know it was his Dad with him. When the Charge Nurse went off, he kept looking behind him.

I was now beginning to get a reputation for 'knowing things' and I was always being asked to read my colleagues' palms, but it got so that I never had a break. Not only that, I was hearing spirits saying things to me, also seeing flashing images of events, so much so that I tried to ignore it all. But when Spirit want you to know something, they don't shut up. It took me a while to learn how to switch off.

For example, I once did a palm reading for our tea lady. But when I looked at her palm, I saw a picture of a young man in uniform; he had a hole in his chest and I could smell gunshot fumes. From my face, she could tell I had seen something bad but I covered it up, saying I wasn't really any good at reading palms. "Oh, yes you are," she said. "You told my friend things that have happened." Well, it must have been by divine intervention that the ward phone rang for me and I excused myself, very relieved. A week later, the tea lady wasn't at work and someone told me that her son was in the Army and had been shot and killed. His mother was devastated and never came back to work.

I do love reading tea leaves, though, and it's always just come naturally to me. I see visions, numbers and shapes, then look for where they are in the cup to know how long it is likely to be before things happen. The cup's regions act as a 'psychic map' for the questioner and the pictures created by the leaves are interpreted according to where they are situated. For me, near to the handle is concerned with business, for example, and the side relates to careers. There's a timescale, too: if a symbol is close to the rim, it refers to something happening soon, whilst images on the side are not so important and the leaves at the bottom represent events further into the future.

There are other good fortune-telling tools, like runes for instance. These come from an ancient Nordic culture; there are twenty-five symbols and together they tell a story and advise us how to deal with issues in our lives. Numerology can be useful in everyday life, giving us signals. Three is the number of pregnancy so, if I see 3.33, I know I shall soon be hearing of someone being pregnant. The number five relates to a new home and so on. Over the years, my favourite spiritual tools have been Tarot Cards and crystals.

After a while I was allocated to a Children's Ward, again on night duty. A little girl aged five was admitted with meningitis and her parents sat with her. They had fallen asleep around 3 o'clock when I saw a pale blue light shimmering above the little girl; it looked like the face of an angel, looking down at the child and smiling. The strange thing was, it had golden ringlets just like the little girl. The little lass was deteriorating fast so I rang the emergency call bell. Doctors came flying into the wards, straight out of bed with hair sticking up and shirts on back to front. The girl was transferred to another specialised hospital.

Her parents told me that the girl was a twin and that the other one had died at birth. I knew then that her sister had come to help her get well. That little girl is now grown up and a nurse herself. It's strange how life turns out – many years later she was allocated to me as a student while she was training. She said, "I remember you from when I was in hospital with meningitis. You saved my life. And I felt my twin sister was with me, too, I was so poorly." Well, yes! Her parents called into the ward to thank me as well, but really it wasn't me: I just noticed that shimmering blue light and went to investigate and check on the girl. It was her spiritual sister who saved her.

I took the nursing exams and passed as a State Enrolled Nurse. We were known as 'the bedside nurses' whereas the Registered General Nurses were deemed to be more academic. It soon became very noticeable that the RGNs would give the SENs the mucky, mundane jobs to do like cleaning the sluices, running errands and making the patients' teas. I had not worked hard and studied, passed all my assignments and practical assessments, to be allocated the mucky jobs, no way. Anyway, why should I do them while the Auxiliary was sitting having a cup of tea with Sister in the office? Yet there was nothing I could do about it since Sister had her moles, her favourite tale-tellers…

"I am off," said Vera, of the same mind as me. "Are you coming with me?"

Jobs were scarce at that time because there were so many newly-qualified nurses who had secured places on wards of their choice. I was still thinking about what I wanted to specialise in, too. Vera discovered that Swallownest Psych-Geriatric Hospital was advertising for night duty nurses so we applied and both got jobs there.

We didn't often work together but, when we did, we laughed the whole shift. On my first night, I thought immediately there was no way I could stay there, it was so spooky! Yes, I was okay with seeing ghosts and spirits but this place was buzzing. I was allocated to a men's ward of six beds where some of the patients just came for respite. Mr Burns always came for four days from Monday to Thursday; he suffered from dementia and could sometimes be violent, and his wife was also very ill with cancer. On Wednesday night around 3 o'clock, I saw Mr Burns get out of his bed and waddle along to the toilet; he had a very distinctive walk and he wore big brown trousers with red braces holding them up. I did wonder why had he had got dressed just to go to the toilet. After five minutes I went to check he was all right but the toilet was empty and I was sure I hadn't seen him come back because I was watching for him. So I got up to check his bed only to find there was another man there… I searched the whole ward and even the adjacent women's ward.

"What's wrong?" another nurse asked me, so I said I was looking for Mr Burns. "He died yesterday," she told me, "he just collapsed on the toilet." I decided not to say anything because they would think I was crackers. So, Mr Burns had come back as a ghost to visit the toilet? I know some patients do get obsessive about going to the toilet but this really took the biscuit.

A couple of months later I was on a women's ward along the corridor. Six ladies were all asleep so I thought this should be a good night, which it was until four o'clock. Clara had been institutionalised all her life, having been raped by a local landowner when she was a maid in his house; she got pregnant but they took her child away and she was put in the workhouse. She had bouts of screaming for her child and the only thing that would calm her down was a doll, her 'baby'. I didn't know where the doll was kept so I rang another ward to ask.

But then Clara suddenly became very quiet. When I started to walk down the ward towards her, I couldn't believe my eyes: there was a Matron standing at the end of her bed with a German shepherd dog spirit. Then the ward door was flung open by a nurse bringing Clara's doll. She said, "I thought you said she was screaming?" Luckily for me – so I didn't have to explain – she then started again.

After everything had quietened down, the next thing I heard was a shout, "I've sh… my knickers!" Oh dear, it was one of the violent patients we had to keep sedated because she was an alcoholic; she was in the hospital because she had thrown a television at her husband when he would not give her a drink. I rang for help and it took four nurses to change and clean her up while she cursed and spat at us, wrestling with me and biting. Fortunately, I had kept my tetanus jabs up to date.

How did they deal with this daily? I liked working there but after all I had trained for two years and here I was up to my eyes in faeces, being bitten and spat at. I knew then that I had to leave. The staff working there were marvellous at their jobs but I had not really been welcomed apart from by two auxiliary nurses. Kate had been there years and she helped me fit in better, telling me about the patients because I had no idea what they suffered from and why they were there.

That evening, she brought me a cup of tea and left it on my desk. I heard someone shouting and swearing so I walked down the ward, but it was just an old dear dreaming; I went back for my tea – the cup was empty! None of the patients could walk and there was only me there, the ghost Matron and her dog… Did the ghost get thirsty? Later, I told my mother the story and she said, "I was in that hospital with rheumatic fever in 1930. There was a Matron there who used to bring her dog to work so the children could play with him." But I still didn't know where my tea went.

Gradually I got used to the patients and would study their notes to find out a bit about their lives before they had become mentally ill. Six months in, I had learned to do what the rest of the staff did: there was no point arguing about all sorts of things with patients who were stuck in their ways, best to go along with whatever was happening. Still, I wasn't happy and the final straw came one evening when I was on a ward with six beds and patients who were extremely violent. I gave them their drinks at nine o'clock.

There was one lady who liked to wear a sort-of crown; perhaps she thought she was the Queen. She called me over and said, "Servant, bring me the commode." I replied that she could get out of bed and go to the toilet since she was perfectly able to walk; after all, she would wander around all day pointing at people with a stick that looked like a kind of dagger. For some reason, the staff let her keep it under her pillow; she said that she needed it for protection because people were trying to steal from her. She started shouting and swearing at me so I gave in and fetched the commode to her beside. "You may go now and start the breakfast," she said. When I turned my back, she poked me with the stick shouting, "Security! Arrest this woman, she is stealing my jewels." The Charge Nurse who arrived told me that the lady had been the housekeeper at a stately home; she still thought she was there and that we were her servants.

This wasn't for me.

3

God's Waiting Room

I went back to where I had started but this time as a qualified nurse. It was strange walking back onto the unit where all the same staff were there, including the Grey Lady!

At six o'clock one evening, I was doing the drugs round when Mr Dent called out that he wanted a word with me when I had finished. I replied, "About fifteen minutes, okay?" But when I looked at him, I had a bad feeling about him – maybe the bronchoscopy had shaken him up but he looked peaky and his aura was grey. I had come to recognise the colours around people and could read what was going on with them, knowing what condition their body was in by seeing their auras. Mr Dent had come into the Chest Unit for investigations and not because he was poorly; the only reason for being admitted was that he was breathless when walking up hills. He'd had his bronchoscopy that afternoon and as the results are written up straight away I thought I'd look at his notes before going back to see him. They read, 'Bronchial tumours and widespread metastases. No treatment, only palliative care.' I walked back to his ward with a heavy heart. What was that smell? Oh, it's white lilies – how I hated that smell and still do to this day.

"I am going home today, nurse, so I wanted you to thank the Matron who sat and held my hand last night. She had a big red cross on her dress and a large hat. Funny though, she didn't speak at all, just held my hand. I felt so relaxed and safe." He sounded so happy, I couldn't tell him what I knew so I just agreed to tell her. Later, the Consultant came round and delivered the bad news to Mr Dent and his relatives, who were shocked because he had not been ill. He asked Mr Dent if he would like to stay in hospital.

"Yes I would, the nurses are marvellous!" I was standing there thinking, 'Please don't mention the Matron with the red cross…' Of course, there were no nurses in the hospital like that, only the Grey Lady. I went off-duty knowing that I wouldn't see him again. Next morning the ward was in chaos, with bloody needles and swabs, an ECG machine and a defibrillator all beside Mr Dent's bed. The Night Nurse apologised to me for the mess and said that he'd had a cardiac arrest at five o'clock but they couldn't save him. She was surprised by how relaxed he'd been, though, and it was as though he knew he was going to pass over. He had even left some money under his pillow with a note that read, 'For the wonderful care and attention given to me. Especially the nurse with the red cross on her dress.'

I was glad to be back on the Chest Unit. It was a happy place to work, even though we had a lot of deaths and it became known as God's Waiting Room because a lot of patients had cancer.

Elaine was thirty years old and a Primary School teacher, tiny like a little mouse and so beautiful. She had been coughing up blood, a bad sign especially in someone so young; she had her bronchoscopy and even without being told I knew that she was dying. Sometimes I would wheel her outside into the sunshine and we would talk about things.

"Do you believe in angels?" she asked me. I told her that, yes, I had seen them. "I dreamed about an angel last night," she said. "He had on a green gown and had lovely blond hair, like I would like a boyfriend to have – if I had one. He put his big fluffy white wings around me and it felt so good."

I felt really upset listening to her because I recognised her description of Archangel Gabriel, one of the 'angels of death' who escort our souls to Heaven. I went off-duty but couldn't stop thinking about her, leaving instructions that a doctor should talk to her parents and make them aware of how poorly she was. The following day I was on the late shift and Elaine was still with us, thank goodness. Around nine o'clock all the patients were in bed, but we heard children singing All Things Bright and Beautiful. It was coming from Elaine's private cubicle and was so loud that I went down the corridor to ask her to turn the music down; then the scent of white lilies hit me. 'No, please let her be okay,' I thought. When I opened the door I saw three Victorian children singing and Elaine was smiling.

"The children have all come to see me, nurse!" I knew then that I had to inform her parents; psychic or not, nurses know when the end is near. She died an hour later. I went to the funeral and, as her coffin came into the church, the hymn being played was All Things Bright and Beautiful. That's what Elaine was and I shall never forget her.

There were several more sightings of the Grey Lady and she flitted around the ward as if she owned it. It got so that we started to ignore her and what once had been a big issue was now normal. But on one occasion she did us a good turn…

A very posh lady was admitted. She was very off-hand with everyone as though it was our fault she was on the ward. Her husband came with large bunches of roses and smoked salmon for her tea, fussing over her. Then after he had gone, along came her boyfriends, two of them coming at different times. Her nightdresses were beautiful but hardly suitable for hospital, very low and revealing! Her cubicle was like a florist's with boxes of chocolates and perfume too, though she never offered any of us a chocolate and hid everything from view. Either she was very selfish or she didn't want her husband to see them.

One Sunday we were sitting on the veranda and talking with patients and relatives; things were more relaxed at weekends and relatives could stay longer and have their tea with the patients. Posh Lady did not speak to anyone, though, and questioned everything we did. But we were an easy-going bunch and just got on with things.

I went to give out the drugs when I saw the lady standing at the end of the corridor, although I don't know how I recognised her because it was just a skeleton walking towards me… I don't scare easily but I just stood there mesmerised. The figure changed back into Posh Lady and I asked if she was all right.

"No, I am bloody well not," she replied. "Can you keep that nurse out of my cubicle? She keeps coming and just stands there without saying anything. I want to report her." I asked her to describe the nurse. "Grey dress, white pinafore with a red cross on it – and she smells very sickly." I asked how many times she had seen her. "Twice, and you had better sort it out because my husband is a police officer, a sergeant, and I will be reporting this to him. You nurses think you can just do what you like!"

"Has she hurt you in any way, or perhaps touched you?" I asked. "What are you reporting her for?"

"Well, just standing there she scares me. And by the way, I have seen you having cups of tea when on duty." I told her that we were short-staffed so we didn't go out to have a break, that's why we took it on the ward. I probably shouldn't have said this but I was so angry with her and couldn't stop myself continuing: "We have been very discreet about letting your boyfriends come out of hours to visit you – do you think I should report that?"

I knew I'd gone too far and was sure she was going to report me, but in fact she changed overnight; she became really nice to everyone and even asked if she could share a cubicle with another lady. Naturally, I asked her why she had changed.

"It's that nurse. She came back and said, 'Pray with me,' and she held my hand. I felt overwhelmed." It was the first time the Grey Lady had spoken to a patient.

A week later, the lady's results showed lung cancer with spinal metastases. By now, she had changed into a lovely woman, even helping to give out teas to other patients' relatives. Soon she was packed up ready to go home and asked me to escort her to the toilet as she was now so frail. We linked arms and I walked up the corridor with her, both of us smelling the scent of white lilies.

"Don't think I'm daft, nurse," she said, "but I'm sure that nurse with the red cross was not my imagination. You call her the Grey Lady, don't you? Is she a ghost?" I thought 'This is going to be tricky' but I just smiled and said that, yes, sometimes she comes onto the ward but, in any case, when a patient is on a lot of medication that can affect the mind and the way we see things. She went home and died two days later. After a while, some chocolates arrived for us with a letter saying, 'I knew she had come to warn me that the end was near. It was the Grey Lady that people spoke about. Thank you all, you are amazing.'

A lovely lady, eighty-five years old, was admitted from a nursing home with lung cancer, coming to us for palliative care. We fussed over her because she had no relatives and never had a visitor. One afternoon we were serving teas and when I tried to enter Mrs Frank's cubicle I found myself blocked by some sort of 'invisible cobwebs'. Looking inside, I could see that someone was sitting beside Mrs Frank's bed, holding her hand. I told another nurse that the lady had a visitor but the door seemed to be blocked, so she tried but couldn't get in either. Ten minutes later I went back to find the lady smiling. She said, "My time has come, nurse. My dead sister has just been to visit me." Mrs Frank passed away peacefully the next day. I learned that those 'invisible cobwebs' are a kind of spirit curtain, put in place when someone is ready to pass over.

Spirits often seem to recognise that I can see them. Early one evening, I was starting the drugs round when I realised that the pharmacy box had not arrived. The medication was needed urgently for one patient so I called the pharmacy who said they were short-staffed and asked me to go over to collect the box. I ran over there and on the way back I passed the big house at

Oakwood Hall that used to house wounded soldiers in WWI and where the Grey Lady had been a nurse.

I heard a voice behind me say, "Hello, nurse." I was a bit scared because it was dusk and this area was isolated: your mind runs away with all sorts of ideas – who was he, did he have a knife and was he going to harm me? I turned round to see a soldier in battledress. My uncle was in the Army so was it him messing about? No, this soldier only had one leg and he had a rifle in his arms.

Then I realised that he was a spirit, and obviously Earthbound; this sometimes happens when death is sudden and the spirit wanders about until it is helped to 'go to the light'. I greeted the young man and he simply replied, "Blown up," before vanishing. When I got back, I told my colleagues and they just laughed, saying that they'd also seen him looking through the window. Perhaps he was looking for the Grey Lady, or 'our Elizabeth' as we sometimes called her; she seemed to be very fond of soldiers and the patients she visited on our ward nearly all had military connections. I thought that these soldiers needed help instead of just roaming the hospital grounds so I contacted the priest who regularly came to the ward and told him what I had seen. He said, "Don't get involved, they will go eventually." This soldier was seen by other people for a while until eventually there was no further mention of him.

The Grey Lady was such a regular visitor that all the staff knew about her, even if they hadn't seen her themselves, and one September I had a particularly close encounter. It had been a horrible shift, there had been two deaths on the ward and I was looking out of the window watching for the mortuary truck to arrive so the bodies could be removed. I was thinking how fragile life is and my thoughts went to my Grandma Mac and how much I missed her. A tear dripped down my face.

As I stood there, I felt someone come up behind me and put an arm around me; the reflection in the window was of a lady in a grey coat, wearing a poppy. Why wear a poppy in September? I turned around to find no-one there so walked along the corridor checking the cubicles for a woman in a grey coat wearing a poppy, but there was no-one of that description to be seen. I then went to make the patients' teas and saw the same lady pass the kitchen door. But when I ran out there was no sign of her so it dawned on me that she could be the Grey Lady. One of the older nurses told me that, yes, she sometimes wore a grey coat.

"Well, she just put her arm around me," I said. The nurse replied that the Grey Lady liked to be able to comfort people and obviously thought that I needed a hug. A hug from a ghost, who would believe it? I unlocked my office door to find a poppy lying on the desk… I was the only one with the keys so it seems that the ghost had also left me a present. This kind of rare event is called an 'apport'. Perhaps the Grey Lady knew that I loved visiting the WWI battlefields and that sometimes the soldiers would appear to me, so she left the poppy to acknowledge that.

I was now ready to further my chosen speciality, so I asked for a transfer to Central Treatment Rooms to learn about wound care. I had set my mind on getting a degree and was determined to achieve it. At first, I was apprehensive about going into a new environment since I had left a place that was so friendly.

Central Treatment was really busy. All the procedures were done in cubicles: wound care, procedures like lumbar punctures, minor operations, gynaecological care, endoscopies and so on. I loved it. Some of the nurses were nice, others not so much, but nurses come in all sorts of guises and I learned so much. One Sister was especially helpful and I could see an orange glow outlining her body, an aura that means intelligence; she was an amazing teacher and I always knew she would go far in her career. She did not believe in spirits or anything connected with spirituality so I never said anything to her. I had arrived with a reputation and some of the staff knew about my psychic readings, but I tried to keep a low profile.

I was left to work on my own after three months and was allocated a Student Nurse on a weekly basis, although I always seemed to get the awkward ones. Hopefully, Sister felt that I was more patient than some or that I was a good teacher! We were allocated our patients according to which procedure we were doing that day. I was often doing chemotherapy cytotoxic instillations, using drugs to destroy cancer cells by inserting a catheter into the urethra to instil the medication. We would have to wait with the patient in case of leakage or a reaction to the medication, so we got to know our patients very well.

One day, I was very tired because at two o'clock that morning I'd had a dream in which a blue and white 'plane burst into flames as though a bomb had gone off. I woke my husband and told him but he said it was only a dream and to go back to sleep. The date was 21st December, 1988. I was sitting and talking with my patient when he commented, "Isn't it awful, that 'plane blowing up this morning?" I hadn't seen the news and said I didn't know anything about it, so he told me it had been a blue and white Pan Am 103.

I nearly fainted. He asked if I was okay and I replied that I was just tired, but then he came out with the strangest thing. "You saw it didn't you? I am a Spiritualist and I saw the same thing." This man would come once a week and I looked forward to his visits; I always gave him his treatment and we talked about spirituality and such things. When it came to his last treatment, he didn't turn up and a phone call from his wife told us that he had passed away very suddenly the night before.

I had taken a course on treating leg ulcers so was allocated most of these to be redressed in the department. Rose was a very large lady who had bilateral leg ulcers, one venous and the other arterial; she was also diabetic so extra care was need when redressing her ulcers. I was not allowed to do this for her because

I knew her personally (it still puzzles me why you cannot do your friends' or relatives' wound care). When she came into the department on her bed, I looked over to her but saw her mother's face, not Rose's…

She called out to me to come over and gave me a crystal angel, saying, "I might not see you again, they are sending me home." A voice in my head said 'She is not going home.' This was odd but by now I was used to such occurrences. Straight away, I could tell that her ulcers were infected and there was a deathly scent of lilies. I couldn't see her after she had been treated because rooms had to be closed for an hour to cleanse the air and the walls washed in hexetidine to control infections. She was taken back to the ward after her treatment and I popped up to see her at dinnertime. But all the cubicle curtains were closed on the ward, doctors and nurses were flying in and out of the curtains, and I just knew what had happened. Above Rose's bed curtain I could see the silver cord hanging down. The Charge Nurse told me she'd had a cardiac arrest and they couldn't save her. I was very upset and felt in my pocket for the crystal angel she'd given me, thinking back to when I had last seen her. I still have that crystal and I think of Rose often.

Hannah was a nurse whom I worked with; she was very bubbly and always laughing, married with two children and also career driven. One day I was working with her and a doctor doing minor operations, standing side by side, when she banged her arm. She said "Ochs!" and when we looked down at her arm there was a massive bruise. I thought to myself, 'There is something wrong here' and then I heard a voice say, "It's my granddaughter – she will soon be joining me." Of course, I couldn't say anything.

I had applied to take a BMedSci degree in Professional Nursing practice and had just started, in 1999, when the door opened and Hannah walked in. The tutor introduced her and said that she'd be joining us this term. She came to sit next to me and immediately I could smell death. At break time we didn't go to the dining room with the others and just sat and talked.

She told me that she was dying, she had leukaemia, but really wanted to finish her degree. Her constant tiredness made things difficult for her. Now, I wasn't the best academic in the room but I offered my essays to Hannah to help her because there was a lot of research involved.

She was becoming weaker and then was admitted to hospital for a bone marrow transplant, but unfortunately she caught pneumonia and passed away. We were told that she would have her degree awarded to her posthumously and an Award was set up in her name for the best student of the year. I know she will be looking down smiling, pleased that she got her degree, and she has come through to me a couple of times since then. But I am not disclosing what she said as it was private, for someone else.

Central Treatment Rooms were being rearranged with staff allowed to follow their specialities. A new Ward Manager came in who had attitude problems and of course there were the usual cliques. When I think back, I feel sorry for many of them because of course I could read their auras and was never fooled by their behaviour. I watched how some of them bullied other staff but I had got into enough trouble in the past, speaking up for people only for them to turn their backs on me, so I kept quiet.

One nurse, however, would always lighten the mood. She was quite a big girl, with long dark hair and very astute, so funny that she made everyone laugh. I loved working with her. One time I told her the colours of her aura and said that big changes were coming for her. The next time I saw her, she was very slim and glamorous!

4

Why Do We Do It?

I got my degree and the Nursing Officer asked me to set up a Teaching and Assessment Course for students to be tested on their knowledge of wound care. Well, unfortunately not all nurses are angels, they can be jealous and spiteful like everyone else and a lot of obstacles were put in my way. I started to think of leaving but I loved my job so I stayed, and the next sad story is why I changed my mind.

I was allocated a Student Nurse and at the start of the week I was waiting for her because she was late. Then she practically ran into the department apologising that she'd had to take her sister to school. Astur was a tiny little Somali girl with great big brown eyes, a beautiful soul.

I went through all the competencies she had to achieve and as I got to female catheterisation she became tearful. I told her not to worry, that I would guide her through the procedure, and she gave me a watery smile and said "Okay." But I felt an overwhelming sadness around her and however much I tried to shake it off it wouldn't go away. As she was speaking about what she wanted to achieve, I had a vision of a primitive hut with several women

35

around, all dressed in brightly coloured clothes with matching headdresses. There was a red aura outlining the hut that indicated 'danger' to me and I knew this was connected to Astur. Was she in danger? So I made extra sandwiches and yoghurt and we shared them sitting outside the hospital. She said she was very grateful to me for helping her and my Grandma's words came to my mind: "Be kind to people on the way up because you'll need them on the way down."

Thursday came and the catheterisation procedure was the only competency left to do. She said, "I don't feel well, can I do it another time?" I put my bossy hat on and said "No." Then she started to sob and as she did so I saw a double of Astur standing at her side with a hand on her shoulder. Well, I always looked after my students because I'd been there and experienced what they were going through; sometimes qualified nurses forget that and treat students as a nuisance. So I said, "Let's go into the office and talk about this. You can tell me what's wrong." I made her a cup of tea – with a tea bag, not with leaves this time, although even so I don't think I would ever have realised what Astur was going to say.

"My sister Hibaaq was twelve years old and we were twins. She had been playing in the water with a boy of about thirteen when our mother saw them and assumed they were boyfriend and girlfriend. We were quite developed, going into puberty. Mother pulled her out of the water and instructed my oldest sister to fetch the medicine woman, a local midwife.

"There were six women holding my sister down whilst they did a genital mutilation on her. She was screaming but they wouldn't let me comfort her. We went back to our hut and Hibaaq just lay on the bed moaning. She had a fever and was in pain and our mother was crying for what she had done. The women outside were shouting that she had an evil spirit in her and she should die."

As Astur was telling me this, I could see Hibaaq standing at her side and smiling, but I didn't want to interrupt. Astur went on to say that her sister developed sepsis and died soon afterwards.

After the family had laid her to rest, an angry mob of women confronted them saying that they were all evil, so they ran to the nearest police hut for safety and later managed to come to England as refugees. Astur had promised her sister in spirit that she would help people who were suffering so she studied hard to become a nurse. What a story! I understood how brave she was and vowed that I would always be there for her and help her get through her exams. Shortly afterwards, I told her that Hibaaq was standing next to her and would guide her. She turned to me, smiled and said "I know, I can smell her, she smelled of oranges." Astur became more confident then; she gained her degree and moved to London to specialise in gynaecology.

All through my nursing career I have prayed for angels to help me on my path. I can always feel when angels are around because the place is calmer and so am I. Archangel Raphael is the healer. And there were so many times when I needed that extra angelic guidance, mainly in dealing with other healthcare staff!

I had begun teaching wound care at other hospitals and I loved the work; I had found my speciality. But back then hospital consultants were gods and some had a bluntness that made me want to run and hide when they were talking to patients. I requested to go into theatre to watch surgery being performed so as to get a better idea of what the patients were suffering from and how best to treat their wounds. There were horror stories of consultants throwing used instruments onto the floor (I thought that would go down well in the Infection Control Department) and shouting at nurses, complained about anything and everything.

I was standing across from an orthopaedic surgeon who was doing a hip replacement when a spirit lady appeared at the side of him, looking at the young man who'd had a motorbike accident and had broken his femur. The surgeon was being very rough, using something that looked like a power drill to shape the bone. The lady looked straight at me and telepathically said, "He'd better not hurt my boy." Yes, a spirit mother watching her son's operation! A moment later the surgeon whipped around and said,

"Who just hit me on the back of my head?" The anaesthetist said that he was the only one behind him and didn't do it, so I knew it was the boy's mother – he was being too rough with her boy so she whacked him.

Another time, I upset a consultant who was a very big man, loud and narcissistic. A young man was being prepared for abdominal surgery and was lying naked on the operating table. I was feeling very uncomfortable with this, as were some of the student nurses, because this man's dignity should have been respected. But the consultant was just laughing with the nurses about something that happened the night before. I thought, 'Right, I am going to put a sterile towel over the man' and I heard an inner voice say "Do it." The surgeon turned on me and said, "How dare you touch my patient – haven't you seen a prick before?" He pulled the towel off the patient and people were sniggering behind their masks. At first I felt embarrassed, then a power surged through me: when I am mad, my eyes flare.

"One day," I said, looking him straight in the face, "you might have to go through what this young man is going through. Would you like it, having everyone staring at you naked?" He clapped his hands sarcastically but now no-one laughed or sniggered, so I carried on, fuming. "What does the Hippocratic Oath say? We should uphold ethical standards and treat the patient with the upmost respect and maintain their dignity." He grinned and replaced the towel.

Next day I was on the Orthopaedic Ward, checking a wound, when he walked in. He stood next to me, saluted and said, "My god, you've got some spunk to challenge me. By the way, nurse, my new mantra is 'You must maintain the patient's dignity'." Many years later, after he had retired, the same surgeon came into my department with a urinary problem and had to have a catheter inserted into his bladder. I was fully trained in that procedure and could have done it, but I got a male nurse to do it instead. As the man left the department later, he called out to me, "Thank you for maintaining my dignity, nurse!"

I was asked to go to a different hospital to demonstrate a new wound application, maggot therapy. This was a trial for a medical company. When the maggots arrive they are like tiny hairs; when they have done their job, de-sloughing and debriding, they eat the necrotic tissue leaving the healthy skin alone so that when the dressing is removed they have become fat little grubs. I set up a PowerPoint demonstration to explain how to use the maggots.

Doctors, consultants and nurses all came to watch. In the middle of my demonstration, a voice piped up, "I won't be using those disgusting creatures!" It was a consultant who worked in surgery, sitting there with one leg across the other and pretending to yawn. I ignored him and he again tried to be clever. "How much are you getting paid to push this thing on us?" I replied that I was a nurse in tissue viability and was not paid to sell the product; and, incidentally, the company's reps got double my salary. But he wouldn't stop and then said, "My wounds don't get infected, so we won't be having this in the hospital."

Well, I had done my research and he had made a fool of himself because I could point out that his hospital in fact had a large quota of infected wounds. I went on to say that if he was not interested in giving the product a try then he should leave the room and not try to embarrass me: I knew my stuff and taught it every day to nursing students and doctors. The room went quiet as he got up and left, then everyone started clapping. (What was it about me and consultants? I am quite laid back until I'm challenged but I seemed to fall out more with them than anyone else.) I was writing up the day's report, not saying anything about the surgeon, when he walked into my office.

"I have come to apologise, nurse, for being off-hand." As he spoke, a spirit lady appeared at his side, clearly his mother. He sat down and continued, "My mother had an infected abdominal wound and she died three weeks ago. I couldn't do anything, nothing worked, and today brought everything back, so I am sorry."

I wondered whether I should tell him that his Mum was there with us, but assumed he would think I was crackers and report me. Then he looked at me and said, "I smell lily of the valley, my mother's perfume, a lot and sometimes I think I can see a flash of her." So my question was answered. I looked him in the eye and asked him whether he believed in an afterlife. Surprisingly, he said that he did.

"That's good," I said, "because your Mum is here with us and I have a message for you. Are you ready for it?" At first, he laughed and said it couldn't be true but then, after some hesitation, asked me to tell him. "Your Mum is saying that you knew her kidneys were failing and that's why the wound broke down." He nodded in agreement but, as if to test me, said that this could apply to almost anyone, so I carried on. "Before your Mum died, she'd asked to be buried wearing a necklace with the letter M for mother on it, and she says 'Thank you' for doing that. She also says that those stupid, fluffy pink slippers you bought her for a laugh… your wife wears them now."

His face was ashen now and I thought he was going to faint so I got him some water. He shook his head and asked me how I knew all those things. "You look normal but you talk to spirits – where did you learn all this?" I told him that I was a hereditary psychic medium, the ability passed down from my Grandma Mac, but that first and foremost I was a Nurse Tutor and that paid my wages.

"Our paths were meant to cross today," he said. "I can sleep easy now, knowing my mother knows that I did all I could for her." So it turned out to be a job well done. There was a big order from him for maggot therapy, a glowing report of my demonstration, and a bunch of red roses was waiting for me when I got back to the hospital, meaning that I was teased for having a secret admirer!

I returned to Central Treatment Rooms and to a new manager who didn't want me going to other hospitals to teach wound care. I was to stay in the department and teach our students. The way that things were changing frustrated me because, now that I had my degree, I wanted to teach more widely and this was like putting a lid on a bubbling pot. So I went to see the Nursing Officer and said I would like a change and to learn about Traumatic Wounds.

She asked me to go into the Accident and Emergency Department to teach the new techniques since the staff there were quite stuck in their ways. I had already designed a Kardex system of wound care products describing what should be used to treat different kinds of wounds. There are also many different sorts of bandages used for specific purposes and, for example, putting a compression bandage on a leg ulcer can stop the blood flow and lead to amputation.

So I moved to A & E with the Nursing Officer's parting words ringing in my ears: "I want you to make sure that they take notice of what you say." She might as well have said, "I am throwing you to the lions." I was not well accepted. The Sisters had been in A & E for so long, a particular routine had been established and when I turned up one of them actually said, "We didn't want you." This was a time when Sisters and consultants took tea together, and I was an outsider who was scrutinising their knowledge. Well, I'd had more aggravation than this in the past and I was determined to do what I was sent for.

There was some hostility but the younger Sisters were nice and gradually I became accepted because I had a very good knowledge of wound care – and no-one liked doing the dressing clinic anyway. In time the doctors also accepted that I knew my stuff. The department began to change, no more cosy chats with the doctors, and one by one the staff left and new people came in. I loved traumatic wound care, everyone had their favourite speciality, and we all worked well with a good team spirit.

A new post for a Sister was advertised and the senior Staff Nurses assumed that one of them would automatically get the job. But they didn't, a Sister came into the department from outside and there was a lot of animosity towards her. That was just how I had been treated so I took her under my wing. One day she said to me, rather forlornly, "Do you think I will ever find someone to love?" I told her a little about my 'other talents' and went on to reassure her that, yes, she would meet him soon and he would be tall, dark and handsome and wearing green. She scanned everyone wearing green for a couple of weeks! Not long afterwards, we were on a late shift together when the red Emergency Phone rang, meaning that a seriously ill patient was arriving. The emergency call went out and doctors came into the department. We had just started doing CPR when the door flew open and there stood a man in theatre greens, tall, dark and handsome. Sister just stood open-mouthed and looked from him to me. They later married and had children.

When you work in A & E you have to get used to experiencing some very sad and emotional events – and making some very difficult decisions. Triage (originated during the Napoleonic Wars by French doctors) is a particularly high skill that requires not just medical knowledge but personal intuition too. Theoretically, there are five categories in assessing a patient, from 'immediate treatment necessary' to 'non-urgent'.

For example, I once triaged a man who was intoxicated; his eyes were bloodshot and he had fallen and grazed his hand. He had difficulty speaking, vomited on the floor and complained of a headache. So this is just a drunk, isn't it, a Category 5 for a wounded hand? Yet I felt that something wasn't right with this man and asked him whether he had banged his head when he fell. He mumbled, "Yes." As far as I was concerned, he was now a Category 1 and required urgent treatment. It turned out that the man had sustained a sub-arachnoid haemorrhage (a brain bleed) and he died next day.

When the Red Phone rings we know it's bad and to expect an emergency. Paramedics give us the details in advance about what has happened and the patient's condition, then we wait at the door to take over from them and continue the patient's care.

The paramedics told us that they were bringing in an eighty year old lady in who had fallen against a red-hot radiator. She was badly burnt and very distressed. Her husband had gone shopping to buy her a new nightgown and some cakes, but she had fallen out of bed and become wedged between the bed and radiator for an hour. She had a third-degree burn that had gone through the skin and affected the deeper tissues.

We transferred here to the resuscitation room because of her distress, gave her pain relief and treated the wound with a cream used for extreme sunburn, to soften the charred skin so that a graft could take place. But then I got the familiar tingling feeling in my hands that told me this lady would not survive due to the shock. We were moving her to a side ward when a man arrived, shouting for his wife. I explained what had happened to her and he pulled out the most beautiful nightdress I have ever seen, pale green and embroidered. He wanted to put it on her immediately but of course that would have messed up the burns treatment. Moreover, I knew privately that she was going to die, so we could put it on her then.

"She has dementia," he said. "I was only out for an hour and she was asleep when I left." He sat beside her singing nursery rhymes and holding her hand. I felt really moved by his love, especially when the scent of lilies then hit me like a smack in the face. A doctor and I took him into the relatives' room and told him that she was very ill and may not recover. What should we do if she had a cardiac arrest? It turned out that she had previously signed a Do Not Resuscitate (DNR) form, and her husband said, "I have signed one as well. I don't want to live without her."

We made our way back to the cubicle where he held her hand again until she died, then stayed with her for hours until eventually his son came to take him home. The following day the Red Phone rang again. An eighty-five year old man had been found collapsed on the floor by his son; he had a slow pulse, we couldn't get any blood pressure and CPR wasn't making much difference. He was the husband of the lady who'd died of her burns the day before. There was nothing we could do and he died an hour later.

Most nurses do cope well with death. Watching someone pass over can be very daunting as you wait for that last breath, holding your own breath, wanting to breathe for them. Then it hits you that they have gone and your professional head takes over, no matter how you feel; showing your emotion is not going to be helpful for anyone. Some relatives will continue to sit beside the deceased and talk to them for ages, holding their hand and even making bizarre comments. I remember one man saying to his Dad, "I will take your ashes to the bottom of the sea because I know you hated water." What could I say to that?

However, I have an incredible gift and it is very special to be able to see a soul rising and someone coming to guide them to Heaven. It is both amazing and comforting to watch a patient's facial expression change when they are ready to pass over and know that someone has come for them. Of course, the end of an earthly life is sad, but I know that their suffering has now ended and they are at peace. Phones and bleepers may be going off, doctors are doing ward rounds, hectic life is carrying on in every department, but we have complete peace behind the curtain, awaiting that special moment when our patient is reunited with their loved ones on the other side.

I watch for the signs in each new patient. If the silver cord has broken then I know that the patient has already died and many times I have seen the soul rising from the body just as they came through the A & E door.

It was three o'clock in the afternoon when the Red Phone rang and the paramedics told us they had a young lad who had hung himself about fifteen minutes earlier. He had been found straight away by a man walking his dog. The paramedics were on the scene fast and had him given CPR, hoping that maybe there could be a chance to bring him back. As soon as they brought him through the door, I knew that he'd passed over but in such circumstances I keep quiet – it is not my job to certify that people have died, I only do it spiritually.

The doctors carried on doing CPR and we all tried what we could but he had gone. I volunteered to look after him. In attempted suicides (there was a note in his pocket), everything must be left intact: the drains and needles, catheter lines and paperwork, everything labelled to be sent to the coroner.

I was washing the lad and, as I walked to the sink, I felt a rush of wind in the room and a fragrance that I couldn't describe. It also became freezing cold. I thought my mind might be playing tricks, but I covered him up so that he wouldn't get cold, putting a shroud on him and making sure the marks on his neck were covered so that relatives who came to see him would not be even more distressed. I was washing his muddy hands when he spoke to me in my mind: "I want me Mam." The suicide note had said that he couldn't cope without his Mam and he wanted to be with her. Then I realised that the fragrance and cold wind could have been signs of his Mam's presence.

"I hope you are with your Mam now," I said to him, "and at peace." As I turned back from writing out the identification wrist band, I saw clearly a woman standing over him; she had long black hair and was wearing what looked like a white wedding dress. She was very beautiful and the boy certainly looked like her, with the same black hair and blue eyes. She looked at me and simply said, "He wanted to be with me."

I sometimes wonder why I have this gift that is so often revealed in moments of heartache. There are many things I cannot reveal about Spirit communication – things that would not be considered appropriate in the circumstances – and that saddens me because it could mean the world to someone who had lost a loved one tragically. In this particular case, my head ruled my heart because I had a professional job to do. That doesn't mean I don't care.

The lad's father arrived with other relatives who were distressed and wanting to see him, which of course in a coroner's case is not allowed. Besides, he still had all the paraphernalia attached to him. But we were a caring bunch in A & E so I thought I would break the rules, with my manager's permission. I asked the father just to identify his son and promise me that he wouldn't touch anything, then I stood outside the room for a few minutes out of respect for the family. Well, if he kissed his son that was all right with me. He told me that the boy had tried to kill himself before, wanting to be with his Mam who had died of cancer three months earlier; he'd had treatment but was determined to find a way to get to her. He was only sixteen, with his whole life ahead of him. When the father left, despite his terrible sadness, he said, "Thank you, nurse, you are an angel."

That's when you know you're in the right job.

5

Spirit All around Us

I was seconded to take the A & E Emergency Trauma Course at
Lodge Moor Hospital in Sheffield, an old spooky place that has
housed many disciplines including patients with mental illness. I
made friends with Mary who was on the same course.

On Monday morning we were all assembled in the Great Hall
and the man in charge was telling us what the rules were. I had an
awful feeling about him; then, as I watched, his body changed to
a skeleton, not a good sign. There was also a spirit man standing
beside him who seemed to be about the same age. I whispered
to Mary, "That man is very ill." She asked me how I knew that,
was I psychic or something?! But even she could smell the scent
of death, which she described as like white hyacinths and really
strong. The following week, there was another tutor in the man's
place as he had passed away suddenly. Everyone gasped except
me and Mary.

Our classroom was at the end of a long corridor. One day we
were going for our break when I saw smoke at the other end of
the corridor and a man standing there in a leather flying helmet
and jacket. I asked Mary if she could see him and she couldn't,

but she could smell the smoke. I found out later that a 'plane had flown into Lodge Moor Hospital in 1955, killing a lady. The pilot had survived so I don't know who the spirit was that came through. Maybe it was him, now passed over but Earthbound because of a sense of guilt.

Another ghost actually sat in our classroom! She had a green nursing uniform and a white pinafore with blood on it but she vanished as soon as we entered. I learned that a man called John Timmons had once murdered twelve women, one being a nurse, and had been a patient there when Lodge Moor was a psychiatric hospital.

Soon after this, I was seconded to another hospital where it was so busy that no-one had any time to talk – the Red Phone just rang and rang. One day I was told that people involved in a road traffic accident were coming in: six people had been injured, one a pregnant lady. A doctor said, "She's your case." At first, I thought I couldn't do this, I was only on secondment in a strange hospital where the other nurses hardly spoke to me… then my determination kicked in and I told myself it would be good experience. Well, it was – but not quite as I had expected.

The lady was eight months pregnant with internal injuries, conscious but losing a lot of blood. The doctor warned me to be aware that she may lose the baby; he examined her and wrote down 'No foetal heartbeat'. Then the most amazing thing happened. I clearly saw a Chinese spirit, a man wearing a white coat and a gold earring, put his hand on her abdomen. The baby moved. The doctor and I were both stunned – for different reasons – and she had a baby boy an hour later by Caesarean Section. I have often wondered if it was her guardian angel looking out for her and the baby, and anyway I am sure he was a spirit doctor.

My next secondment was in a smaller hospital where the nurses were more welcoming. At about 3 p.m. one day a lady came running into A & E with a baby around nine months old; the baby was blue so we rushed him into Resuscitation. Rather than doing the Heimlich Manoeuvre (a First Aid procedure for dislodging an obstruction in the windpipe) that might have damaged the child's ribs, I turned him upside down and made him cough. A piece of plastic Lego fell out. Then a strong scent of bluebells wafted in and, when I looked up, in the corner stood what looked like an angel, one of those little cherubs with chubby cheeks, so then I knew the baby would be all right. The mother admitted that she had been so fed up of his crying she had emptied the box of plastic Lego bricks onto the floor for him to play with, then left the room. Most parents will know the feeling of having a screaming baby and trying everything to pacify them; that's why she did it, never thinking that it could have caused the little lad to lose his life.

In another hospital, I was in an Observation Ward and the place was strangely quiet; all the nurses had vanished. I had to wait for a porter to transfer a lady to another ward and when he came I asked him where everyone was. He looked a bit uncomfortable, then said, "They're playing with an Ouija Board in the end room – just knock on the door because it will be locked." At that time, I wasn't aware of 'bad spirits' that might try to trick or hurt you and I was curious, never having used the Ouija Board before. I was also disappointed that the other nurses hadn't asked me to join them, but maybe they'd thought I would report them because I was on secondment and not one of their team. When I came back from taking my patient to the ward, they were all standing around talking about what had happened; one of them noticed me and invited me to join them next time for 'a bit of fun'. I said I would love to… although I had a bad feeling.

The nurses had the table set out with numbers, letters, and the words 'Yes' and 'No' on pieces of paper in a circle and an upturned glass in the middle. There were four of us sitting around the table and the atmosphere was tense and a bit scary. We all put a finger on the glass and one nurse asked if there was any spirit there who wanted to give us a message. There was silence, then the glass started to move around from one letter to another, spelling out 'C-e-d-r-i-c'.

"Is that your name, Cedric?" asked the nurse. The glass moved to 'Yes'.

"Who are you?" The glass spelled out...'d-e-a-d'.

"Have you got a message for anyone here?"

The glass now started to move very fast, spelling out the name of one of the nurses in the group, and then...'d-i-e'.

The nurses all screamed and then the papers lifted up into the air and fell to the floor as the glass fell off the table and smashed. I thought to myself 'This is not good' and we should have learned our lesson, but a week later we were around the table again. This time we got the name of a cleaner who had worked in A & E and had passed over two years before.

"How did you die?" asked one of the nurses. The glass spelled out 'brain bleed' which made the group very excited.

"Are you happy in Heaven?" The glass spelled out 'f... o..'!

"You were a lady," commented the nurse. "I never heard you swear like that."

I had a very bad feeling about all this and said that we should leave it now because it didn't feel right. Then I heard a voice in my head saying, 'Tricked', and I told the others that someone or something was playing a trick on us. Of course, I then had to own up to being psychic. The papers were still on the table and the nurses had their fingers on the glass; it started to move again, spelling out 'tricked', and then we all heard a muffled laugh. Everyone made for the door, frightened to death.

Ten minutes later, I heard a large bang and the fire alarm went off, coming from the kitchen. I ran in, got hold of the fire extinguisher and sprayed it onto a plug that was in flames. Soon everyone was in the kitchen asking what had happened and the nurse who had instigated the Ouija Board 'game' said, "I was going to make us all a cup of tea and when I switched on the kettle it blew up." She had a nasty burn on her arm and they never used the Ouija Board again. But that wasn't the end of it...

A year later, I was back in my own A & E when the Department Manager asked me to look after a nurse who was doing a course here. I asked her name but at that moment she walked in – it was the same nurse who had set up the Ouija Board in that other hospital.

When we were on our own, she asked if I remembered when 'Cedric' had spelled out 'die' and the name of one of the other nurses. I could hardly have forgotten because she had screamed so loud we had all jumped. The nurse told me that, yes, she had died in a road traffic accident six months before. She was very upset and felt guilty that it had happened because of her: if we hadn't played around with the Ouija Board she would still be here. I reassured her that it was nothing to do with that; her time was up and there was no connection.

We were to do a night shift together the next week so I promised to try and bring her friend forward during our break. That night, the department was empty so I told my colleagues I had to do this nurse's assessment and didn't want to be disturbed unless the Red Phone rang. I had brought my Angel Cards, the ones I was using then to communicate with Spirit; on these cards there are also specific messages. I asked the nurse to take three deep breaths and to pick four cards from the deck.

The first card out was 'Hello from Heaven' so I knew that her friend would be coming through; I could also smell her fragrance, she wore Miss Dior all the time. I could sense the nurse's negative thoughts and doubts so I asked her please to have faith in me and her friend. She agreed that it was all very strange to her but it was fine to continue with the message from the cards she had picked.

Archangel Azrael: 'Your loved ones in Heaven are doing fine. Let go of worries and feel their loving blessings.'

Archangel Chamuel: 'He brings peace – remember the good times.'

I could feel her friend coming closer now and heard her voice, so I told the nurse her friend was here and that she had a message for her: "It's not your fault. I was looking in the glove compartment and crashed into a tree." The nurses confirmed that this was true.

51

Archangel Jeremiel: 'Overcoming difficulties – the worst is now behind you and the challenges of the past are now behind you.' The spirit nurse came through again and said, "I will be at the party." Her friend replied that they had booked a Christmas party and all of them wished she could be there because they missed her; some of them even thought they had smelled her perfume.

"It was me," came the response. The reading was beginning to flow now and I thought that if I used the cards the link might be broken, so I asked if it was all right for me to carry on clairvoyantly. She was already sure that I had 'got her through' so I suggested that she ask some personal questions that would really prove it was her friend, and she did that. Before long, a knock on the door interrupted us and we had to go back to work; as we got up, I asked her if she was happy with the reading and feeling reassured.

"Happy?" she said. "I am over the Moon, thank you so much. If I get some Angel Cards, do you think she will she come through to me?" I answered that, yes, she could buy them but that she needed to join a Mediumship Development Course, to bring out any psychic ability she might have – and that she should never use an Ouija Board again because they are dangerous.

Most people would never in a million years think I am a medium because I do seem so normal. Well, it is normal to me and I use my gift with the best intentions to help people. So when I get to Heaven I want a seat next to the Big Man! I've always found it strange how people's perceptions change once they know I am a psychic medium. It can go one of two ways – either they are constantly asking questions about the spirit world or they try to avoid me!

The next day back was very busy. The Red Phone rang because a lady had collapsed in the street; the paramedics were doing CPR as they brought her in and she was still alive. The young doctor taking over the CPR caught hold of the red beads she was wearing but they broke and went all over the floor. I picked them up and put them all, loose, in a pot in a desk drawer. Then as I turned around I came face to face with an old spirit man who said, "I've come for her – I told her I would." I looked at the ECG reading and noticed she was in asystole – she had died.

Two weeks later, a lady came into the department looking for her mother's red beads. I told her they'd been broken and I had them in my drawer, but when I opened the drawer I saw that they were all threaded back together. I asked around but nobody knew anything about it; after all, who has got the time to thread a necklace in A & E? Another mystery.

It can be especially challenging when mentally ill prisoners are brought in. One was a known violent offender, in prison because he had nearly killed someone. This time, he had tried to slit his wrists. There were two policemen with him, a doctor and me, and we were stitching his wounds when he pulled away and thumped me in the back. I sustained two broken ribs and was off work for six weeks. There were no apologies although the police should have restrained him better, and I could not claim compensation because he was mentally ill and didn't know what he was doing.

One of our regular mental health patients was 'Sharpie', a man of around thirty years old. We always knew what to expect when the paramedics informed us that Sharpie was on his way to us. Still, we were very professional with him. He had fallen in love with a young student nurse and would ask for her to treat him every time, so it was up to me to tell him that she was no longer here and a male nurse would see to him. This was appropriate anyway – we called him Sharpie because he would insert sharp things down the side of his penis. Over time there had been a scalpel, a needle, a razor blade, a steel comb and a pair of tweezers, each of which had to be removed in Theatre. Unfortunately, we learned later that he had tried to put a pair of scissors down there, caught a vein and needed a penectomy.

At Christmastime, I always volunteered to work the night shift since my own kids were grown up with their own families and some of the other staff had little children of their own. It's always sad around Christmastime to see the usual patients coming into A & E; often it's relatives bringing their old parents in, saying they have been vomiting or coughing up blood. I sometimes suspected that this was so the younger ones could go away, or they just found their parents a hindrance to them.

We decked the corridors with holly, put up a Christmas tree and carol singers visited the wards to sing for the patients. I always found it ironic when they got to A & E singing Silent Night because it was anything but that for us. Why do people expect emergency treatment for minor things like an ingrowing toenail, a toothache they've had for three days or a scratch on their arm? At this time of year there were four nurses and two doctors on the night shift, all experienced except perhaps a House Officer who had only been there three months and was very nervous and unsure of himself. In our situation, it's not about doctors being in charge of the nurses, it's teamwork that matters. Patients always want to see a doctor whereas there are Emergency Nurse Practitioners who have probably worked in A & E for years and have taken specialised courses.

One Christmas Eve, the department was packed and we all mucked in doing what we could to get the list down. We were doing well until one o'clock when the Red Phone rang: there had been a big fight in the town centre with five badly injured. They all came in by ambulance, laughing and joking. One lad had severe lacerations due to someone smashing a glass in his face, and I carefully picked out twenty-two pieces of glass (which had to be saved for evidence).

"You remind me of my Mum," the lad said. I asked him what had happened to him, why someone had attacked him with the glass, and I suddenly realised why he'd said that about his Mum because I could feel a woman's spirit presence near me. He went on, "My Mum died on Christmas Eve in here. She had a heart attack."

I checked his name and then remembered his mother. She had been quite young and we'd tried so hard to save her with the defibrillator and taking turns with CPR, but it was too late. What he said next really shocked me.

"I caused an argument with someone so I would get hurt and have to come to A & E on the night my Mum died."

I fully understood where this lad was coming from. In the Kubler Ross model of 'five stages of grief' it is highlighted that people often want to be in the place where their loved one died; this lad had clearly not reached the stage of acceptance. I was torn – should I tell him that his Mum was with him or should I not? No, it's not appropriate to blurt out something so raw to someone who is obviously still grieving.

This was turning into a difficult night. We had treated thirty patients, the walking wounded. We still had a man on a trolley who had fallen down drunk and fractured his femur; he was waiting for the orthopaedic doctor to come, but the doctor was so tired he had fallen asleep on a couch in X-ray. (Doctors often work incredibly long hours at this time of year, covering for their colleagues so they can have Christmas with their families.) We had given the femur man gas and air so he was fine, on his own little trip. At 3 a.m. we had a coffee and a sandwich and a big joint sigh of relief because the department was nearly cleared.

The Red Phone rang again. The paramedics were bringing in a lady who has jumped off a motorway bridge and was still alive. We got the Resuscitation Room ready and put out an emergency call to doctors from surgery and orthopaedic medicine. Obviously, the lady had multiple injuries but I could see that the silver cord was still intact, although when I saw her I couldn't believe how she had survived – her hair was pushed back over her skull and she had broken nearly every bone in her body. She looked around forty years of age but otherwise we had no information about her so we just started to treat her.

Then someone found a card in her pocket, reading, 'I do not want to be resuscitated'. There was a name on the card so the police made contact and it turned out to be her husband, who came rushing into A & E.

"Where is she?" he shouted. "I'm going to give her a bollocking. I told her not to go out." I told him that she was unconscious and took him to the relatives' room where he said he was going to call his girlfriend! It did not look good for the lady. Then the man started banging on the door saying that he wanted to see his wife and tell her how sorry he was… it didn't go down well when I replied that she was very ill so he had to sit in the other room until his girlfriend came. The doctor called out that the lady was going into cardiac arrest and he tried three times with the defibrillator; I just watched and waited, and then I saw her soul leave her body.

I had to go back to the relatives' room, where I found her husband sitting and holding another woman's hand, to tell him that we had done everything we could but it was bad news. He stood up and pushed me over, rushing straight into the Resuscitation Room where he saw his wife on the table before the doctor could block his view.

"I feel strange…" he then said, starting to sweat and clearly having pains down his left arm. He was having a heart attack so now we were treating a man who'd had an affair behind his wife's back, making her so distraught that she had committed suicide by jumping off a motorway bridge. We learned that she had found out by opening a present meant for the other woman, finding some very beautiful lingerie with a note inside. She had confronted him and he had admitted the affair; now he would have to live with the vision of his poor wife as she lay dead on a hospital table.

Even that was not the end of my Christmas Eve. At five o'clock, the Red Phone rang again. An elderly lady, a Type 1 diabetic, had drunk a bottle of whisky and was now in a coma; it was the first Christmas without her husband. She was moribund and barely breathing when she came into A & E and the doctors got to work on her, trying to bring her round, but it was no good and she died. I told the doctors I would sort everything out for them because they all looked shattered; they would certainly remember their stint in A & E this year. As I was clearing up and putting the lady's belongings in a bag for the coroner, something caught my eye, a flash of a man with a white beard. I thought I must be hallucinating from lack of food because he looked like Father Christmas. The lady's sister had been visiting her and when she came in she commented that this time of year had been particularly bad for our patient because her husband had always played Father Christmas for all the children…

Sadly, there are more overdoses and cut wrists around Christmastime. Perhaps it's due to the loneliness of people who cannot cope without friends and family. We also see a lot of elderly people every year, who want to be in hospital for Christmas so that they have some company and a good Christmas dinner; many of them go home the next day. We had a regular homeless man who would come into the department pretending he'd had a heart attack. We would put the ECG monitor on him and fortunately it always showed that he was fine, but he would be kept in overnight for observation. He would arrive every year on Christmas Eve, knowing that he would be treated well, have some good food and, if the nurses had time, a bath. Naturally, we all felt sorry for him and staff would bring him extra food and clothes and we even had a whip round for him. We do see a number of homeless people, very happy to wait three hours in A & E where it's warm and there are free drinks.

Everyone has extra-sensory perception to some degree and people either accept it and perhaps try to develop it, or ignore it and hope it goes away. Not many people can cope with the gift of being genuinely psychic. I sometimes feel that fate – or Spirit – has taken a deliberate hand in directing certain patients to me because of this. From time to time, there's a happy ending.

The paramedics brought in a lady who had taken ten paracetamol and was hearing voices, so it looked like she was schizophrenic. I was the only nurse free to see her. We went to a cubicle so that I could do a stomach washout there and I asked her why she had taken an overdose. She told me that she had been seeing visions and hearing voices that gave her information about other people, which made her think she was losing her mind.

I got on with the job of dealing with the paracetamol (luckily there's a drug that protects the liver if it can be given within an hour), then we sat down for a chat. The lady was quite astute, very well dressed, and I noticed that she was wearing an angel necklace.

I knew that this lady did not have schizophrenia and I understood why she was talking about the voices and visions, but she was just frightened by it all. She told me that she could smell different fragrances in her home and often heard a voice saying, "Hello, it's John," (her late husband's name). The angel figurines on her home altar had been moved around. One day, she had left the gas on and then heard someone shout "Fire!" I smiled at her.

"It's not funny, nurse," she said.

"No," I replied, "but I will let you into a secret. I also hear voices and see visions. You just have strong extra-sensory perception – you are gifted, being able to hear voices and see visions. It is a fantastic ability to have though, yes, when you don't understand what's happening to you it can seem scary. Look, you will have to be admitted to the Medical Ward for observation but when you go home I want you to buy two books so that you will understand what is happening." I gave her the titles and the next day she came into A & E to thank me.

Two years later, I was working at a Psychic Fair when I saw, across the room, this same lady all set up to do psychic readings herself. I went over to her and asked if she remembered me.

"Remember you?" she smiled. "I will never forget you. You saved my life and if it wasn't for you I wouldn't be sitting here. Is there anything I can do for you, please just ask?"

"Well, yes," I said, "there is one thing. Please don't pinch all the clients!"

6

Care in the Community

I spent a period with a District Nurse, working in the community. It was a very cold and foggy day when I met her and she told me there were five new patients and ten regulars. On the way, she filled me in on their histories and said my A & E experience would be helpful. I looked at her, puzzled.

"No kidding," she said, "just wait 'til you see some of them." We pulled up outside a very shabby looking house; the lace curtains were dirty and didn't fit the windows and the garden was completely overgrown. I felt an overwhelming sense of sorrow looking at all the debris around the house too. The District Nurse explained that Mr Young was bedridden and living alone; he had no family, only four dogs which – as I soon discovered – did their 'business' all over the house. A carer came in twice a day to prepare meals for him, feed the dogs and clean up some of the mess.

Mr Young was a diabetic, dependent on insulin, and he had diabetic ulcers on his feet that needed dressing every day, which is why we were there. The front door key was under a plant pot since he couldn't get up to open the door, and when we went in the smell took me aback, a dirty, earthy smell mixed with dog

59

poo. The gentleman was lying on his bed with the four Yorkshire terriers, which all started making a mournful screeching noise. The state of them was heart-breaking and I could see straight away that Mr Young was very ill and should really be in hospital, but he refused to leave his beloved pets. It is sad to know that so many people are suffering like this in their own homes.

The District Nurse was looking very concerned and we could both smell the scent of pear drops, which indicates diabetic ketones, a dangerous condition. She asked the man if he was feeling poorly today.

"Yes. I am dying. My wife told me." When we were out of earshot, she remarked to me that he got confused and that his wife had in fact died six months before. She went into the kitchen to prepare his insulin while I started to take his dressings off. In conversation, I said to Mr Young that his dogs were lovely and I offered to come over one day when I was off-duty to groom and bathe them. "It's all right," he said, smiling, "my wife looks after them." This kind of situation is where things can get a bit tricky for me, since the District Nurse for one didn't know about my psychic gifts and I never broadcast it. But as I turned away to place the dressings in a bag, I saw an old lady wearing a blue dress and sitting on the bed.

"Hello," I said, "who are you?"

"I told you, nurse," Mr Young said. "It's my wife and she's come for me."

The lady looked perfectly real and solid but when I reached out my hand it went right through her. She just sat there and watched me working for quite a while. "How long were you married?" I asked and she replied, "Fifty-five years and I'm still looking after him. He's coming with me now."

The District Nurse gave him his insulin while I made him some tea and then we chatted about his dogs. But before long I noticed another familiar smell, that of death, so I said to my colleague that I would like to stay with Mr Young for a while. She looked at me and just smiled, saying, "You know, don't you?

Okay, I'll call back for you when I've finished the rounds." She was one of the best, no questions, just a knowing between two nurses.

Mr Young's breathing was now laboured and I knew he was slipping away. I wanted to reassure him so told him that I had a friend who is a foster carer for dogs and she would find them new homes. At that moment his wife reappeared, smiled and nodded to me, saying, "God's angels."

"My wife is here to take me now," the gentleman whispered, and I held his hand as I watched his soul leave his body. How wonderful it is, I thought, that his wife of more than fifty years would come to take him to Heaven. The District Nurse came back with a doctor to certify the death and we did the last offices and informed the undertaker. Then the last thing we could do for this lovely man was take his dogs to my friend, who in time found them new homes.

The following week we were allocated more patients. It was a rural area and without a Satnav we often got lost! One new patient lived with his elderly mother but she couldn't cope with him now that he'd been diagnosed with a brain tumour and was deteriorating very fast. It was both a mental and a physical challenge because he had aggressive moods, and we were warned that he was very unhappy about us coming. This didn't worry me because I knew I could handle myself – after all, I had protected my mother from many beatings by my father, and my uncles had made sure I could handle myself.

The house was a mess, very cramped and we could hardly move for pizza boxes, dirty chip cartons and mucky pots. I felt so sorry for this little old lady who was stick-thin and had massively swollen ankles; her aura was lilac and green with patches of red and I knew she had tried her best with her son – but now it was time to get help for herself. We heard a loud bang from another room and then a shout.

"Mother, come and pick me up!" We rushed into the other room to help but could hardly believe what we saw: he was very obese, just sitting on the floor, and expecting his poor mother to lift him up on her own every time this happened. She told us he wouldn't let anyone else touch him. And I had a bad back too... We managed to get him back into his chair as he spat at us both and told us to, well, go away. I told him that we were there because his Mum needed a bit of help and if he didn't let us do that we'd have to call an ambulance to take him to hospital.

"Satan's bitch!" he said, but I've been called worse working in A & E. "You're after my money," he went on. "My Dad told me. So get out of my house." I asked him where his Dad was and he put his hands together and started reciting the Lord's Prayer... my heart softened. Then I noticed there were a lot of religious ornaments and pictures in his room, and a burning candle next to an angel figurine to one side – a real fire risk! This situation called for some creative lies, I thought, even if that meant I didn't get to Heaven myself, so I knelt down next to him and took his hands.

"We have been sent to help you and your Mum," I began. "Your Dad is unhappy that she has to lift you by herself when you fall." He looked me calmly in the eye.

"Are you an angel, then?"

"Yes," I said, "we are two angels sent to help you." Then, as I got up, the spirit form of his father appeared, looked at me and smiled, so I carried on. "I can see that you like angels. I have special angels helping me, too." His Mum chipped in now, "Oh yes, he loves the angels and he talks to them. Archangel Michael is his friend, you know, and says he has seen one in a white robe who keeps coming to visit him."

I told the gentleman that it was important he help us so we could wash and do his dressings, and he looked from me to the District Nurse and back again, saying he was sorry that his illness made him say bad things. We understood that, of course, so carried on doing our nursing chores while talking to him and his Mum.

"My Daddy is here," he suddenly blurted out. "He says I must behave and not be a naughty boy. Can I go to bed now?"

I wanted to cry. I am not normally an emotional person – my friends and family call me the Ice Queen – but I felt so sorry for this man. He had owned his own business, had a wife and kids, but lost everything because of his illness; only his poor old Mum stood by him. At this moment, I could feel his father's presence in the room and there was a smell of cigarettes, so I realised that this man's time was coming to an end; he was having angel visions and his father was coming through to take him. He pulled at my sleeve tearfully and handed me some rosary beads and two rose quartz crystals, saying, "I want you to have these, they mean 'love'."

I realised now that the family were Catholics and wonder whether his Mum knew he was near death and may need a priest. These circumstances are difficult, if people are Catholic but not aware they are dying and need the last rites; this is very important in their faith. He was deteriorating fast in front of me and instinctively I began to tell him about my Grandma Mac and how when I was a child we would make fairies out of felt and take them to the Catholic church to be blessed…

"Mum," he suddenly called out, "can you call the priest for me? I want to talk to him. I don't feel well." I breathed a sigh of relief and told him that we would come again in the morning to help him get up. "I won't be here," he said calmly. "My Daddy is coming to take me to Heaven. I'll meet all the angels there." As if by an extraordinary angelic intervention – although it turned out that his mother had sent a note to the priest earlier that day – at that moment a knock came on the door and there was the priest in all his regalia. His mother must have had some idea that he might be ready to pass over.

She asked us to stay so we sat and watched the priest doing his work. I could see his father at the side of the bed and there was a shimmering light above him and a beautiful face looking down on the scene. We then carried on with our visits and learned that he passed away early the next morning. Later we received a lovely card, addressed to 'The Two Angel Nurses', from his Mum who said that she was selling up and going to live abroad.

So many people are really suffering with their mental as well as their physical health. The reason I am describing their sad stories is to show that there are indeed truly dedicated professionals, such as the District Nurse I have mentioned and the Psychiatric Nurse who comes into my next account, who go beyond the call of duty to help their patients and deserve our respect. Moreover, the Spirit is always nearby too, with patients' loved ones offering their support.

One of my placements was at a psychiatric hospital and there were patients who had recently been discharged who needed further help. One particular lady also had bilateral leg ulcers; she lived in an isolated farm house with her elderly sister so I volunteered to go and redress the ulcers to give the District Nurse a break. I saw this as payback time for all her hard work. The Psychiatric Nurse and I drove around for ages until we found it, hidden away by tall conifers, and it looked really eerie and rather scary, not least because there were dolls at all the windows facing us. The door was opened by a very large lady and immediately we were aware of the smell of infected ulcers.

"She has only been home for two days," said the large lady, "and I can't cope with those sores. But be careful – she may try to bite you." It turned out that this poor lady's mind was disturbed and at times she acted like a dog. There are some situations when nurses just have to take a deep breath and count to ten… This lady even had two bowls in front of her, one with water and the other with food; she was looking at us in a hostile way and making a kind of low growling noise. The Psychiatric Nurse quietly warned me not to go too close in case she thought I was after her food – the way he handled her was quite brilliant. But how was I going to dress her legs if I couldn't go close?

Then out of nowhere I heard a voice say, "Stop that now." There was no-one around and the others didn't seem to have heard it, but I could also feel the presence of a woman who had a smell of malt. Our patient immediately became calmer so I gently asked her if I could help to make her poorly legs better.

She moved the blankets and I could see that she was in a bad way, the wounds were necrotic and the only treatment would probably be amputation. The Psychiatric Nurse kept her calm while I did the dressings and then I went to wash my hands in the bathroom.

Suddenly I felt a coldness and as I looked up I saw in the mirror the image of a woman who looked very much like our patient, so instinctively I said "Hello, Mum." She just smiled and said, "Dying," before vanishing. When I went back into the room I told the lady's sister that hospital treatment was necessary because the ulcers have gone too far, but she insisted that her sister would stay at home and that she would look after her. She surprised me with her next words.

"Anyway, I saw our Mum sitting on her bed so I know she's dying."

It is hard to know what to say at such moments so we agreed that a doctor would call to give her stronger pain relief and that we would call back tomorrow. The following day, all the dolls had gone from the windows; we saw them in a dustbin nearby, along with the two food bowls. The elder sister opened the door for us and I saw the spirit form of their mother standing behind her.

"My sister is in bed waiting for you," she said. "She is ready to die." The room no longer had the smell of ulcers but instead there was the scent of white lilies. The lady sat up for a moment, looked at us both then lay back onto the bed. Her Mum was with her, holding her hand, and this time even the Psychiatric Nurse felt the really cold rush of wind as the lady's soul rose up and away. After all her suffering and trauma, in and out of psychiatric hospitals, it was a very peaceful passing. I did wonder whether we had done the right thing by not admitting her to hospital, but in my heart I knew she would have been in isolation and unable to communicate. It was better to allow her to die at home, with her spirit Mum and caring sister beside her.

At Hallowe'en, they say, the veil between this world and the spirit world is very thin and communication can be easier. I discovered this for myself one night when I was back at A & E.

There was a Hallowe'en party going on in the Doctors' Mess and all the nurses were dressed up in red and black with faces painted like Dracula. Well, I am not a 'party person' so I had volunteered to work and there were four of us on night duty with only fairly minor issues to deal with – until the Red Phone rang. Four teenagers had taken drugs at a party and become ill, one of them critical and not looking good. Some of the staff who had been on their way to the party changed back into their work clothes and insisted on helping us: this is how it was in A & E, it's all about teamwork and supporting one another to help our patients.

The two worst affected youngsters were taken to the Resuscitation Room and I sent up a prayer that they could be saved, but we had no idea yet what drugs had been taken. All we could do at first was follow the ABC guidelines and take blood samples. The first patient to arrive was laughing his head off, totally out of it, and the second one was having serious breathing difficulties although I could see that at least his silver cord was intact. His aura was dark green and flashing, then it became a lighter green so I knew he would live.

The third patient, a tiny young girl, wasn't so lucky. The paramedic was still doing CPR on her but her silver cord had broken and the ECG showed that she was asystolic. Everything possible had been done for her. Did she not make it because she was so small whereas the lads were much bigger and stronger? We took her to a sterile room where a doctor came to certify her death and check for a Donor Card, then I was assigned to do the paperwork and inform the coroner and the police so that the relatives could also then be informed. Circumstances like this of losing a child are very emotional.

Just as I bent down to straighten her arm, I heard low whisperings in the room, it became very cold and someone touched my shoulder – but nobody else could have come in. So there were spirits in the room who must be connected to the young lass; I thought I would just stand back and watch and listen. I was rewarded by the appearance of a young girl and an older woman moving around; the girl looked much like the one who had died and the older woman was making a sweeping movement over the body, exactly like a spiritual healer would.

"Nanan's here to look after you," she whispered and the young girl added, "My dear friend," before they disappeared leaving behind a fragrance that I couldn't identify. (Years later, I recognised it when my daughter bought it for me – it was Chanel Number 5.) Before long there was screaming outside the room as her relatives arrived and I went to find the doctor who, like myself, was totally exhausted by now. Another lad's condition was worsening now and he was a cardiac emergency with the doctors desperately trying to save him. He was the youngest of the group and it was a miracle that his cardiac reading improved when the antidote was given.

By now we had discovered that the drugs were Purple Hearts. This had been popular among the hippy community back in the Sixties but we hadn't come across it since and we were stunned as to how these teenagers had managed to get hold of them. Apparently, a dealer had been selling them cheaply at a disco and it was the first time that any of these youngsters had taken drugs. How wicked that a young girl should lose her life because of this. The dealer was never found.

7

Time for Change

I have been bitten, scratched, thumped and verbally abused. I was getting older and thought it was time to slow down and find a job that's not so hectic. Having worked in four different A & E departments, I knew I would miss their staff (and all the ghosts and spirits that hang around just waiting for someone like me to latch onto) but it's a job for young, fit nurses. I would also miss the patients who made us laugh and even some that made us cry, like the homeless and the abused.

There were a few cases that I shall never forget and that seem to sum up what working in A & E was like for us. For example, there was Mr La La Land, who was away with the fairies – almost literally. He was ninety years old. Every so often, he would get dressed up in his Sunday best, lie on the floor, then ring his daughter and tell her he'd collapsed with chest pain (that old chestnut again, we'd say). And every time he came into A & E he would tell us about the fairies at the bottom of his garden.

But then one day he really did collapse with a heart attack. The doctors performed a miracle and he lived to tell the tale. He told me afterwards that during the real heart attack, he'd seen fairies dancing in front of him and asking him to come out to play. "But my mother told them to bugger off and stop tormenting me," he said. I knew immediately that this time was different to the fairy stories he'd told us before because he had seen his mother. That meant that his time was running out. Sure enough, three days later he was found dead on the floor – he'd had a cardiac arrest.

One Boxing Day it was very quiet in the department until the Red Phone rang. The paramedics told us they were bringing a lady who had fallen out of her wheelchair; she had a fractured wrist but she also had motor neurone disease. My heart goes out to anyone with MND because it is soul-destroying. When the paramedic wheeled the lady in, she had a doll on her knee, a Tiny Tears dressed in a beautiful pink dress. She told me that she'd dropped the doll and when she bent over to pick her up she'd fallen out of her wheelchair. "Do you think I'm silly, having a doll?" she asked me. "After all, I am married with grandchildren."

"Not at all," I replied, "my daughter has a Tiny Tears and she is forty!" The lady said that the doll goes everywhere with her; it talks to her and gives her guidance and much happiness. Most people listening to this lady would probably think she was confused, but I didn't; to me, she was a lovely spiritual lady who was very brave. The X-ray showed that she had fractured her wrist.

"I'm going to put a cast on your wrist," I told her, "because your arm is very thin. You can have a fluorescent one if you like – we have pink, green, orange or blue."

"Can I have the pink one – and please would you put one on Tiny Tears as well? It's to explain to her why I have a cast on." I said I would do whatever she wanted. "The fluorescent one will light up in the dark, won't it?" she asked. "I have been in a dark place for years, but I am looking forward to going to the light now. This will be my last Christmas."

I was a bit stunned but I knew she was a special lady as soon as she came into the department because she had a lilac and gold aura around her. Well, I had never put a cast on a doll before so we had a bit of a laugh about some of the other requests I've had over the years. Then when I was applying her cast I felt a 'whoosh' and my hands started tingling, which often happens when Spirit is around. No sooner had I felt this than a spirit man appeared, wearing an old-fashioned waistcoat with a watch chain. He also had very swollen and lumpy hands that I thought must be due to rheumatoid arthritis, and he showed me a man's pipe mounted on a green marble stand.

"Oh, my Dad is here," the lady said. "I can smell his pipe smoke."

I wondered whether I should tell her that, yes, her Dad was here with her. But I needn't have worried.

"You have a psychic gift don't you?" she went on. I smiled and nodded. "I knew it, you have a purple aura around you."

"Well, you have a very lovely lilac and gold one, so do you have the gift too?"

"I do. So what does my Dad say?"

I described him showing me his pipe mounted on green marble and his rheumatic hands, which she recognised as true about him. She said that she would often talk to her Dad through the Tiny Tears doll, and she wanted the doll to be buried with her. I went on to tell her that her Dad was showing me an old 'Golliwog' with red striped trousers on, and the lady said that this was her brother's toy and he had been buried with it. "There is only Dad here at the moment with you," I said.

"Yes, Dad has come for me. Thank you, it is so lovely to meet you. God bless you." I kissed her cheek and she squeezed my hand and waved as her daughter took her home.

That lady had made my day, she was so lovely despite suffering from such an horrendous disease. Later that night, the Red Phone rang again and the paramedics told us they were with the lady who had fallen out of her wheelchair… She'd had a cardiac arrest and they were too late to save her because she wouldn't let her daughter ring for an ambulance; she'd said it was 'only indigestion'. I just thought she had known her time was running out because her Dad had visited her. She had told her daughter, "I don't want to live like this. I will only get worse. I want to go to Mum and Dad."

A few days later I found myself putting a fluorescent cast on a little girl – she wanted green – and as I was applying it we heard a noise. I looked around and saw that a pink cast packet had fallen out of the cabinet onto the floor. So I smiled to myself because I knew who had done this; she was just acknowledging our conversation.

Then, a couple of weeks later, a little girl came into A & E carrying the Tiny Tears doll, still with the pink dress and fluorescent cast on. "Is that your Nana's doll?" I asked.

"Yes, Nana said to me that whenever I feel down I must talk to Tiny Tears and she will help me like she did Nana." And she gave me a big box of chocolates with a card inside that read, 'Never let your aura halo slip'. The card had an angel on the front; she must have written it as soon as she got home from A & E. I often think of that lady and how she coped, never complaining. She was indeed a beautiful soul.

I was becoming exhausted by the end of each shift and even though I loved working in A & E I knew I had to get an easier job, perhaps a part-time one. So I returned to Central Treatment Rooms – but it was the biggest mistake of my life. The staff had changed, there was a new manager who was spiteful and jealous of anyone who was seen to be getting on in their career, and worse than that was the new Departmental Ward Manager. Everything that I had known had changed and it felt very uncomfortable. But I carried on with my work, taught student nurses one day a week and went with a School of Nursing tutor to various hospitals. One day, just as I was ready to go home, the Departmental Manager said, "You aren't doing that anymore, we need you here." Well, I had taken lots of courses and had a degree to be able to teach, but it seemed that all that was now finished. I thought to myself that I would just settle down, keep quiet and look for another job.

I think Spirit was listening and had 'made plans' for me, though they had a funny way of going about it…

One February 14th, I was on a late shift and we were short-staffed because other nurses had plans for the evening and no-one wanted to change to a late shift. I decided that we would only take in emergencies. The phone rang at seven o'clock and the Ward Sister said they had a very large lady with stinking ulcers that were leaking everywhere so please could I redress her legs? Oh yes, and the maggots were coming through! Talk about testing my patience…

As I've described earlier, we would do trials for drug companies and applying maggots to ulcers was one of the trials I had overseen a while ago. The lady was brought down on her bed and I asked another nurse to come and help me when she had finished with her patient. I thought I would fill the leg buckets while I waited so I could soak off the lady's dressings which were stuck on. The buckets were very heavy and I had to carry them from the sluice. When I had put them at the side of her bed, I asked her to turn her body around and put her leg in the bucket but she couldn't manage it by herself, so I tried to turn her leg (which felt like it weighed a ton).

My back cracked!

I could not stand up. I called to the other nurse who came and helped me to sit down; the pain was excruciating. I took some paracetamol and the other nurse looked after the lady, taking her leg out of the bucket, and I managed to re-bandage her legs despite my pain. It was my day off the next day so I thought I would probably be okay, and stupidly I didn't even fill in an accident form. But I couldn't walk so I phoned the manager tell her what had happened and say I would be off sick; she was not the least bit sympathetic and there was no 'Get well soon' and no phone calls later to ask how I was.

A week later, I was X-rayed to find that I had two inverted discs out of place and a tear in my spine, and after six weeks I was asked to go in to discuss what had happened. Anyone would think I had committed an horrendous crime by the way I was interrogated and it felt like they didn't believe me. I had to get all sorts of letters to sign, to prove this and that, and then I was instructed to go for a medical examination to see if I was fit to return to work.

All this stress from the hierarchy caused me to have a brain haemorrhage. I lost the use of my left side and I talked back to front. Clearly, there was no way back for me – they had finished me off after thirty years of service and no-one ever rang to ask how I was. But there were consequences for the NHS and a lot of rules changed, such as no carrying of water buckets and a new lifting policy. But I still wondered what they were going to do when they were short-staffed: leave the patient with a stinking wound? I wasn't prepared to do that and I paid dearly for it.

When I look back, I know I had a fantastic nursing career. I had been a fifteen year old girl who had to leave school without any qualifications to look after her Mam and her two little sisters, yet I had left nursing with a Bachelor of Medical Science degree in Professional Nursing. It was me who was teaching doctors and nurses how to do procedures, and going to other hospitals to teach wound care to their staff.

And all along the way I had felt a presence watching over me, giving me confidence to move forward with my life, both nursing and spiritually. That guidance was soon to lead me onto a new journey...

It took me a long time to recover from the depression and devastation of losing my career. I had studied until 3 a.m. doing my degree, every day at the library researching and writing. Had it all been worthwhile? Since then, I have recovered slowly thanks to a good support network. I got back the use of my left side although I still have difficulty speaking some words at times. My back is still bad and I have tried so many things to help ease the pain. I've paid hundreds of pounds to a chiropractor, attended the Pain Clinic and had nine caudal epidurals in my spine (injections of steroid), I've worn a magnet corset and a Tens machine, and bought an orthopaedic bed! The problems now are kidney and liver failure due to taking pain relief medication all these years.

There was a purpose to all this, as I believe there is to everything that happens to us. I now began to explore spirituality more seriously and investigate why I could see ghosts and spirit people. My daughter saw an advertisement in a magazine for people who wanted to develop their spirituality, a Mediumship Development Course. (Ironically, I now write on occasions for the very same magazine and others.)

I believe it was heavenly intervention that helped me on the road of my new spiritual career, especially my Grandma Mac. She has always been my guardian angel and I often smell her Blue Grass perfume, especially when I need support. I have since learned that I also have two particular spirit guides – a Native American called Black Feather and a geisha girl, Mateo Oso – who have been with me for over twenty years. I have seen their faces and they each have a characteristic scent, wood smoke for Black Feather and lilac for Mateo Oso.

There's a lot of speculation and misunderstanding about what spirit guides are. It can be hard to believe that you can talk to a spirit being, who answers you and guides you in your life (years ago, people were locked up in asylums for hearing voices in their heads) – until you experience meeting your own guide and receiving their messages. Society is more open now and there is a lot of evidence for the afterlife. Spirit guides are with us all the time, non-physical entities who guide souls through many lifetimes; no-one is without a spirit guide, we all have one or more and they may come closer to warn us of danger, for example. In my younger years I would often smell wood burning in a non-smoker's house, and only much later did I learn that this was Black Feather. I have come to trust him one hundred per cent.

By contrast, I believe that guardian angels are spirits who have lived on Earth, maybe a relative who adopts the role, and they can be recognised by their characteristics or by particular actions they have done. My Grandma Mac is near me, I recognise her presence and that gives me the strength and confidence to carry on working for Spirit.

My wonderful teacher Wendy taught me how to meet my spirit guides through meditation. I would begin by breathing deeply and going into a trance-like state. This can seem scary at first because you feel like you are losing control, which is why we need a good teacher to watch over us and make sure we are okay. Well, I started to see mountains and horses and I could smell wood smoke… and then he appeared to me, a Native American with plaits in his hair, a craggy face and a black feather in his headband. He didn't speak, just smiled and then vanished, leaving his scent of burning wood.

I was shocked! My spirit guide had made himself known to me after all this time. I was cautious at first, I didn't know what kind of entity he was, but I had an overwhelming feeling of trust in him. It is a strange and wonderful feeling when you first make this connection and all sorts of things go through your mind: will he take over my thinking, how will he direct me, how will I know he is who he says he is? So it was now time to find out how he would support me in my spiritual life.

When I am unsure of anything, I call him forward and express my thoughts, asking him to give me an answer, either a 'sign' or tele-pathically. For example, I was contacted by a woman who wanted a reading but everything about her seemed somehow dodgy – the way she spoke and the questions she asked over the phone set alarm bells ringing in my mind. Because I was uncomfortable, I asked Black Feather to give me a sign. A few days later, I walked into my kitchen and a newspaper was open on the floor. This was very strange since no-one else was in the house, my husband was away on a fishing trip and the kids have their own homes, so who had opened the newspaper to that page and left it so that I couldn't miss it? Then I smelled burning wood… I picked up the newspaper to read that a woman had been robbing old folks in their homes; and a few weeks later the woman who had contacted me was identified in the news, charged with those robberies.

How does a spirit do that? Black Feather will always warn me if danger is near. I have four dogs and my daughter and I walk them every day in the same woods. One day we were walking along with the dogs loose when I heard a voice in my head saying, "Danger!" I never question this. So we turned around and went home by a different route. We heard later that four men had been in those woods catching rabbits with their bull terrier and Jack Russell dogs, and two other little dogs had been savaged on exactly the route we had taken. Then I went outside and found a black feather on my garden seat… Yes, I know that many people will be sceptical and say that it was just a blackbird and how can a spirit leave a feather for us? I have learned that it's the synchronicity that makes something like this meaningful – a particular sign at a particular time and place. I knew who this was, telling me that he was nearby.

I have also learned that I have two animal spirit guides, one a black bear and the other one a grey wolf, and I often get a glimpse of them when I am out walking which makes me feel well protected. A very strange 'coincidence' happened when I was working at a Psychic Fair. There was a competition to win a big black Teddy bear by guessing its name; the paper already had forty-nine names on it and there was one space left so I wrote 'Morgan'. I won the black bear! I said to the organiser that it wasn't fair for me to have it and someone else should take him for their kids, but she said "No", he was meant for me. Actually, if I'm honest I really wanted him for myself and he has sat in my reading room for twenty years. My husband said I should give him to a child but I am keeping him!

I learned so much on the Mediumship Development Course. In particular, I had been connecting to Spirit all my life totally unaware that I should protect myself, knowing how to open my psychic senses and close them down. It was shocking to realise that I had always been an open book and any dark entity could have clung onto me, which might explain some of my darker experiences with ghosts.

In case it is helpful, this is my own version and interpretation of how to stay protected.

First, I meditate and ask the four archangels to come forward and protect me; I visualise them standing in the four corners of the room. I take five deep breaths and visualise a golden liquid being poured throughout my body, followed by a white light of pure love. The gold and white light go into every part, right down to my fingers and toes.

Then I use crystals to open my chakras so that I can connect with Spirit.

The chakras are important energy centres within the body and the main seven of them are roughly in a line along the spine, linked to the major organs and glands. I start with the base chakra at the bottom of my spine where the colour associated with it is red, so I use a red garnet to open the chakra. The sacral chakra next is orange, opened by carnelian. The crystal citrine connects with the solar plexus and, of course, for the heart I use rose quartz. The next chakra is at the throat, associated with communication, and there I use blue lace agate to open it. In the middle of the brow is the third eye, influenced by vibrant blue lapis lazuli, and finally for the crown chakra I use my master healer, clear quartz, which connects with all the senses.

Having now opened all the energy centres, I ask Black Feather and any other guide present to come forward and show me what they would like people to know. In my mind, I am shown pictures or I might hear a name. If I am doing a psychic reading for someone, I also ask if any relatives or friends in the spirit world wish to come forward and give me a message for them. This is usually very successful.

When I finished the course, our teacher Wendy had a surprise in store for us and on the last day she said, "Next week, we'll see what you have learned." Arriving at our venue the following week, I noticed a lot of people going inside so I knew that she had arranged a public demonstration – there were around thirty people in the room. She said, "Right, make yourselves ready to show the public how good you are." Five of us had trained and I was first up! I protected myself and asked (or rather pleaded with) Black Feather to come forward and help me. Straight away, a spirit man came forward.

"I am Ted. I passed with a heart attack and my niece is here tonight. Please tell her, I told her that she'd end up with a broken ankle in those high heels."

I was directed to a dark-haired lady wearing a long skirt and I asked her if she could recognise the name of Ted who had passed with a heart attack. She replied that, yes, he was her uncle. When I gave her the rest of his message, she went pale and I thought she was going to faint. Had I got it wrong? Then she stood up and lifted her skirt, showing everyone her broken foot which was in plaster. Everyone clapped, I was elated (and relieved) and my senses were flowing.

A lady, who had come with her son, had been staring at me all evening and I wondered what was wrong... Immediately, a spirit man appeared before me and said, "I am Charlie and that's my wife staring at you. Tell her I'm sorry I crashed her car, but she knows I had a heart attack at wheel." I turned to the lady and said that her husband was here.

"I don't believe in all this nonsense," she said. "My son wanted me to come." I asked her if she wanted this message or not and she replied, "I suppose so." So I passed on Charlie's words and she looked startled. "Well, you bloody well tell him that I now have to walk everywhere." I didn't have to give him the message because he was laughing as he disappeared.

Later she asked me for a private reading; I wasn't actually doing this yet but I thought perhaps this was my opportunity to move forward. I arranged insurance, bought some angel figurines and candles to make the room look nice, along with a very expensive CD recorder. I was now ready to be a professional psychic medium. Still, this was my very first one-to-one and I was nervous all day – what if I couldn't tell her anything? She arrived with a green aura so I thought this was a good start, she had forgiven her husband and was healing.

"Ask that husband of mine," she began, "where is the cash? There was five thousand pounds under the carpet and now it's gone." Luckily for me, he did come through but only talked about his coffin, which he did not like. "Well, I have no money," she replied, "so where is it? I got the best I could, you ungrateful sod." She was beginning to get agitated so I tried to stay calm and carry on as again she asked where the money was, but he just replied, "Gone." I thought she was going to have a heart attack, shouting, "Gone where?" There was no answer now, he had disappeared.

We tried to carry on with the reading but she just wanted to go home, leaving with a red aura. She phoned me two weeks later and told me she had been to four mediums and I was the only one who had been able to bring her husband through. Could she come again tomorrow? But I thought it was too soon and unlikely that he would come again for a while. Then she let me know that her husband had gambled all their money away.

This was a bit of a baptism of fire in my new career and, in those early days, I found some of the things I was told almost unbelievable. For instance, another lady came to see me because she had lost her Mum and was feeling devastated; but she also had an inkling that her father wasn't her real Dad so she came to me to ask what the truth was. Her Mum came forward and gave us a name, which turned out to be that of a neighbour. The woman later confronted the man, who had been her father's best friend, and he admitted that it was true.

"Yes, your mother swore me to secrecy," he said. "Sorry, but I am your father."

It seems that I had to get used to sometimes being the bearer of hard news…

8

A Digression

Looking back to my childhood, I can see how my psychic and spiritual experiences developed. By the time I was twelve years old, at a girls' secondary school, I knew I had the ability to see things that others couldn't but I never told anyone about it; it had become normal for me and I heeded my Grandma's advice to keep quiet.

I had a casual friend called Nina who was small and timid and other girls would pick on her, take her dinner money and so on. I was tall for my age so they never bothered me. One Monday morning I found Nina crying and she told me that some girls had taken her lunch sandwiches from her. I felt I wanted to protect her from these bullies so I found the girls and demanded the sandwiches back.

"Get lost, weirdo, and go back to your little friend."

You've probably realised by now that I will stand up to anyone and this was enough for me to get hold of the girl and take back the sandwiches. I warned them not to touch my friend again or I would report them to the Headmistress; actually, bullying wasn't taken as seriously as it is now, but in any case those girls never came near Nina again. It must have been something in my eyes! After that, we became good friends and went swimming and shopping together, our own little gang of girls with my other friends.

It was the school dance and the boys' school was invited. I was too much of a tomboy to bother with boys, I preferred to build dens in the woods, forage for berries and climb trees. So when a boy asked me to dance I said, "No, but my friend Nina will dance with you. She likes you."

While she was dancing I looked at her face, full of love, but then it turned into a skeleton. Obviously, this was frightening and I knew straight away that something was wrong with Nina. She came to sit down, very pale and breathless although her eyes were shining because the boy had asked her for a date. But she said she didn't feel well and wanted to go home; I went along to make sure she was all right but I had a bad feeling about her. I told my Grandma about her and she said, "She is a very poorly little girl and needs looking after."

Next day I called for her to go to school as we always walked together, but there was no answer. She wasn't at school either and at dinnertime her Mam called me over to say that Nina was in hospital because she'd had a bad breathing attack the night before. She asked if I wanted to come and see her that evening and my uncle took us to the hospital in his car. On the way, her Mam was chatting away and saying that since Nina had joined my gang of friends she was a different girl. Nina was in a cubicle, looking very pale and with bruises on her arms. I asked if she had fallen but she replied that they had just appeared overnight.

Then something made me look to the side of her bed and I saw a figure looking down at her. But this was no ordinary figure, it looked like an angel wearing a pale blue dress. When Nina said, "My Nanny has been to see me and she was holding my hand," her mother looked down at the floor with tears in her eyes. As we left I said, "See you tomorrow, I'll bring you some chocolate" but a voice in my head said, "She won't be here."

We walked back to the car and her Mam was very quiet. She turned to me and said, "Nina's Nanny died two years ago. She has come to take her to Heaven. Nina has leukaemia and it has gone too far – I am going to lose my little girl." The following morning at school Assembly, the Headmistress walked onto the platform very slowly and I knew what she was going to say. Nina had died that morning in hospital. In my heart, I had already known she wouldn't recover because I had seen the angel – the first time this had happened for me. I was so upset to lose my friend; still, I hope I had helped to make her last days happy.

It wasn't long before I had another angel encounter. My mother asked me to take some groceries to my other grand-mother's house, five miles away. On the way back at 9 p.m. I waited for the bus but it didn't turn up so I started to walk home. (There were no mobile phones back then.) I had to go along unlit country lanes and I was rather scared because the killer of thirteen year old Anne Dunwell not far away had not been caught.

After four miles I had not seen anything or anyone but I was aware of a very tall shadow behind me. I dared not look round but it didn't seem like someone was following me because I couldn't hear any breathing or the sound of feet on the gravel as I walked. Then I heard a car coming and a voice in my head said, "Hide!" so I quickly hid in the bushes until it had passed. There were three men in the car and it was being driven erratically, so I thought they were probably drunk. I was glad of that 'message' coming out of the blue.

The car disappeared up the road and now the shadow was again behind me, so this time I turned round – and I saw just a face with lovely blue eyes looking at me. I said, "Thank you" and it vanished.

Grandma Mac was waiting at the gate for me when I got home and I told her that the bus hadn't come so I had to walk home. She replied, "Thank God you're all right. I asked the angels to keep you safe." I didn't tell her about the tall shadow walk-ing behind me to protect me from harm because, at that age, I thought no-one would believe me. Yet many years later I learned that there is a very tall angel, in fact Archangel Sandalphon, who along with his brother Metatron were the tallest angels in the hierarchy. I would like to think it was one of them.

By the time I had been married for three years, I desperately wanted a baby and I cried every month. Then suddenly it happened, I was eight weeks pregnant and I was elated. I went to my Grandma's and Mam's, as I did once each week, calling at the chip shop for our lunch, thinking how happy they would be that I was finally pregnant. I put the chips into the oven and then stood up to make my announcement: "I have something to tell you."

"You are glowing," said my Grandma Mac, but she had a tear in her eye. "I can die in peace now – that's what I've been waiting for." I couldn't believe what I was hearing. "I have cervical cancer," she went on, "but I asked the angels to keep me going until you were having a baby."

I was devastated that she would not be there when I had my first child. She went on to say that I would have a baby girl who would have her eyes – they were a beautiful sea-green – then have a baby boy and that she would come back often to see me. Well, the fish and chips went to waste and I cried and cried. The next day, my mother-in-law said she would come with me to see Grandma. As I opened the front door I could smell the frankincense that our priest was wafting over Grandma, giving her the last rites. I sat holding her hand telling her how much I loved her, when suddenly the bed seemed to move and I could smell the polish that Grandad had needed to use for his club foot. So I knew that he had come for her and the end was near. All the family and friends gathered and eventually I had to go home. Grandma passed away during the night.

I had my beautiful baby girl safely and, yes, she had Grandma's green eyes. Sometimes I would hear her giggling in her cot and I would smell Blue Grass perfume, so I knew that Grandma had been around to check on her. Eighteen months passed and I was now pregnant with another baby. It felt different this time, a difficult pregnancy, and the baby was two weeks late so I had to go into hospital to be induced. I had been in slow labour for three days, but then he arrived suddenly. I was allowed home after six hours and just as I was sitting feeding him I started haemorrhaging… my husband rang for an ambulance and off I went, back to hospital, taking baby with me.

I was put on the Isolation Ward (I have no idea why) and was in hospital for a week having numerous blood transfusions and being fed through a drip in both hands, so it was difficult to hold my baby. Early one morning, the nurse had to go out to answer the phone, closing the door behind her. I was looking down at my baby, thinking how handsome he was, when I felt a cold blast of air and looked up to see my Grandma standing beside the bed. She looked down at my boy, smiling, and then smiled at me so that my heart melted and I got an overwhelming feeling that all would be well. The doctor came to check me out and all was well so I went home two days later. My husband had saved a weekly paper for me and as I was looking through it I realised that the date of my vision had been November 1st, the anniversary of my Grandma Mac's passing.

Some years later, it was summertime and we'd never had a holiday so we booked a flat in Bridlington overlooking the harbour. The kids were very excited and I told my husband to take them out while I unpacked. I had just started to unpack our clothes when I heard a clattering noise from the kitchen and went to see what it was: there was a fish-gutting knife on the floor so I picked it up, put it on the sink, and went back to what I was doing. Then I heard it again, and again found the knife on the floor! This time there was also an overwhelming smell of fish; but, after all, we near the harbour so I thought that wasn't too unusual and I didn't mention any of this to the family when they returned, full of excitement.

Later we went out for our tea and as we were walking back I was looking in a shop window when a gypsy came to stand beside me. She held out her hand and said, "Give me a silver coin and I will tell your fortune." I agreed.

She told me that one day I would receive an honour from a university for my nursing career and that my grandmother watches over me and my family with her beautiful green eyes. Then she added that we would never move from our home (we have lived here for over fifty years now) and said that I have an amazing gift of second sight that would serve me well throughout my life. Finally, she gave me back my money and thanked me for not turning her away!

We got back late to the flat and the kids got ready for bed – we were all in one L-shaped room and I could see their beds from mine. At about 3 a.m. I woke up to find the room freezing cold, and when I looked around I saw a full-length figure standing near my children's beds… she was plump with a bun in her hair and wore a leather apron with a fish-gutting knife sticking out of the pouch. I was mesmerised and couldn't move. She looked down at my children then turned to me and said, "Look after them." Then she vanished leaving a strong smell of fish behind.

In the morning, I told my husband about it all and he agreed that there was a strong smell of fish and the place was freezing cold. "Okay," he said, "pack up and we'll find somewhere else to stay." I got talking to the elderly landlady and told her about the fisherwoman I'd seen. She said she'd heard this tale before, about a woman who had lost her children in a fire while she was out at sea gutting fish. That building is still standing and I sometimes think it would be good to go back, if I had the opportunity, and help the fisherwoman go to the light so that she can be at peace and stop haunting visitors.

Later, we took the kids to the zoo a couple of miles away, to see the animals and have a posh afternoon tea. My son wanted sausage and mash and started playing up so my husband took him over to see the monkeys while I took our daughter into the big house, Sewerby Hall, where there are many artefacts relating to Amy Johnson She was the first woman to fly solo from London to Australia in her plane Gypsy Moth and she died in 1941 when her plane crashed into the Thames Estuary. My mother had been in the Women's Royal Air Force and was a mechanic working on the aeroplanes – she adored Amy Johnson so much that I am named after her.

The room there was very cold despite it being July and a hot summer. I stood with my daughter looking at Amy Johnson's photograph when I heard a voice nearby say, "I froze to death." I turned around to see a whitish, floating shape, not a full ghost, that I felt sure was Amy. Even to this day it has never quite been resolved why her plane just went down into the Thames when there had been no May Day call.

Throughout my life, there have been these psychic and spiritual experiences, from childhood and the early years of marriage to more than three decades of my nursing career. It took a long time to recover from my accident and sad memories of losing my job lingered on, so I asked the angels to help me get better more quickly so that I could start on my new spiritual career.

It was my daughter's birthday. We were both very upset because it was the first birthday without my mother-in-law Flora, my girl's Nan. My daughter had a horse who was stabled a few miles away in the countryside and I went to keep her company while she cleaned out the stable. She came over and put her arm round me as I was just sitting on a wall looking into the distance, when we both saw something in the distance coming towards us. As it got nearer, we could not believe our eyes and looked at each other in amazement because it was a pink balloon with Happy Birthday printed on it! I said, "Your Nan has sent that, wishing you a happy birthday" and it made us feel so happy. Later we decided to go out for lunch at a garden centre and there we saw a rose plant, the last one, standing on its own. It was called Floribunda so we knew then by the name that the balloon had been no coincidence.

Early in my new career, I did a Psychic Fair for an organisation supporting abused women. I would bring their relatives forward, tell their fortune and give each one of them a crystal in a nice little silk pouch. I chose the ladies' crystals depending on how bad their problems were. They were overwhelmed. For example, one lady became very emotional when her Mum came forward to say, "Sorry I left you, I had no choice. They took you away from me." But I am not going to write about any of the other personal stories the ladies told me out of respect for them. Some of the abuse they had suffered is beyond belief in this day and age and the perpetrators should be jailed for their crimes.

Here are a few of the crystals I use, in case they are helpful for you:

- *Strawberry Quartz.* This is a pink variety of quartz used for emotional and spiritual healing. It channels away negative energies and brings peace of mind, calmness and confidence.
- *Green Malachite.* I use this when someone is stressed, for healing feelings of worthlessness or depression and for calming the mind.
- *Snowflake Obsidian.* A beautiful black and white crystal used to bring transformation in a person's life. It especially helps feelings of anger or resentment and encourages changes in behaviour and acceptance.
- *Purple Amethyst.* This is called the master healing crystal because it brings guidance, forgiveness and helps with finding your life's pathway.
- *Beige Moonstone.* A feminine crystal that brings confidence and soothes the inner emotions, especially if one feels worthless. It releases compassion and helps us to love ourselves.

At the end of a reading, I would also ask the client if they would like to ask any questions of the pendulum. There can only be a 'Yes' or 'No' answer, according to how the pendulum rotates, and if it cannot answer the question it will not move. Nearly all of the women I saw at that event, though, asked the same question, "Are you sorry for what you did?" I have three special pendulums, crystals hanging on a fine thread, which I use on different occasions and for different reasons.

1   *Yellow Citrine.* This is a yellow variety of the quartz family. I call her Christine and found her in a very dirty crystal shop, in a glass case that hadn't been cleaned for years, where she just cried out to me. I asked the old shopkeeper how much to buy her and he replied, "The eyes are the window to the soul – you have beautiful eyes and a beautiful soul." With that he took her out of the glass case and gave her to me, adding, "Use her wisely." As I left the shop, I looked back to see that the man had the face of a skeleton so I knew he wasn't long for this world; he died two weeks later. I use Christine when a reading has been quite emotional because she helps to overcome fear and encourages personal motivation.

2   *Lapis Lazuli.* This one is called Luna and she's a beautiful royal blue with flecks of gold. This stone encourages truth and honesty in the written and spoken word. It is also the 'third eye' crystal that connects strongly with Spirit.

3   *Angel Aura Quartz.* This pendulum shines with so many different colours and I call her Angel because I use her when I want an answer from the angels. She is a protector and can also be used in spiritual healing. Some use this stone alongside automatic writing, to bring forward Spirit and help with understanding the writings.

My introduction to pendulums came when I was pregnant with my first child and everyone wanted to know what sex it would be. So I tied a thread to my wedding ring and Grandma Mac said, "Backwards and forwards for a girl, round and round for a boy." The pendulum immediately swung backwards and forwards very fast, and Grandma just said, "Well, we already knew that!"

The pendulum works from the very soul and none of mine have ever let me down. As with any spiritual tool, we must show it respect especially in how we ask a question, which must be clear, because the answers can be life-changing and not always what we want to hear. This is a form of dowsing and we receive messages from the universe through our subconscious mind; crystal pendulums are a great favourite with clairvoyants because they give instant answers while we are perhaps waiting for a spirit to connect. It is important to have faith in the universe and in Spirit, and always psychically protect oneself before doing this sort of work; I always cleanse mine with a sage stick to remove any negative energy that might cling on to it.

People sometimes ask me if they can 'have a go' with my pendulum and then think I am being awkward when I tell them that it wouldn't work for them, only with my spiritual energy. One lady didn't believe me and was very insistent, so I let her try: all three of my pendulums just refused to move for her!

It wasn't long before I was being asked to help people find lost animals using my psychic abilities, and this is where the pendulum is particularly useful. I am a great animal lover, as are my children, and at one time we had two horses, three dogs, two rabbits, one tortoise and two yellow canaries. Why the canaries? My husband just walked in one day and said that the colliery was going to close down and the boss was going to wring their necks, so he brought them home. Any injured birds the family find are also brought home so that I can look after them.

One day, I was on a social media website that was a spirituality group attracting lots of different people who asked each other questions and helped one another. A lady contacted me and asked me to help find her dog, Lucy, who had gone missing while walking with her son in the woods. At the time I had no experience of doing this so I asked Black Feather for advice. I got a map of the area and took out an amethyst pendulum that I use when I need guidance, and called on Black Feather and St Francis, the patron saint of animals, to help me find this dog.

Lucy was a border terrier who loved chasing rabbits; her owner said she had run after something in the woods and her son could not keep up with her. But she also said that Lucy had fits and needed medication to control them, which made the situation even more crucial. I spread the map out on the table, held my pendulum over the area where the dog was last seen and tuned into Spirit. I was shown a dark blue car on a dual carriageway and a man was there holding Lucy. Then I saw an elderly couple in the garden of a terraced house where there was a large sunflower; Lucy was wrapped up in a dog bed. The pendulum started swinging on an area five miles from Lucy's home but alas the family failed to find her. A week later, Lucy came through to me during my meditation and I knew she had died. Still, I felt she had been loved and looked after by this old couple even though I hadn't been able to help as I wanted to.

Another lady contacted me and told me an awful tale. She had left her two valuable Blue Staffordshire terriers in the back of her car at a garage while she paid for the petrol. She'd seen a white van following her but there are so many – she lived in London where of course there are thousands of white vans – that she'd ignored it. But then a man had jumped out of the van, opened her car door, picked up the dogs and had driven off with them. She was distraught and crying, asking for my help. I said I would try my very best.

I got my maps out and called on my guides to start the search, but I never imagined it was possible to find the dogs in these circumstances. Sure enough, the pendulum didn't move at all over the map of London. On the off-chance, I took out a big map that covered the whole country... and the pendulum hovered over Manchester. Surely they couldn't be there? I needed help quickly and sat meditating at my kitchen table, almost in despair, then heard just the one word: "Gorton." Where the heck was that? It turned out that this is the name of an area to the south-east of Manchester city centre. Then my trusty spirit guide said, "High rise", which I presumed meant a block of flats. I phoned the lady to tell her what I'd got, apologising that this was all I could do.

"Right," she replied, "there are ten of us and we're going to Gorton!" I thought what if it's wrong, they'll be wasting their time, but in my heart I knew I could trust my spirit guides. Sure enough, two days later the lady phoned me again. "I don't know how you did that," she said, "but I am so grateful – we've got them back. We went knocking on doors, asking people if they had seen the dogs and eventually a man said, 'Yes, I know who has them but it will cost you.' So we phoned the police and they came with us to the flat. A woman answered the door and I could hear my babies barking. They were there, just where you said they'd be. The people were going to sell them to a breeder." Two days later a large cheque arrived from her but I told her there was no charge for finding animals and it would please me if she made a donation to an animal sanctuary I know, which she did.

After all these years, Spirit still surprise me with what they can show and tell me.

A lady told me that her three cats had gone missing. She said, "We live in the countryside and they go off to find mice, but they always come home for their food around the same time. They've been missing for three days now. Please can you do a reading for me at my home?" As soon as I went into the house, I knew the cats were dead because they were there with me in the kitchen, brushing against my legs. So I had to tell the lady I was so sorry but they weren't coming back.

She started to cry and then asked me if I knew how they had died. I was shown a blue tractor that had been cutting the hedge-rows, running over the cats. I told her that it was an accident and the farmer has buried them on his land. To my surprise, she said, "My Dad has a blue tractor, I'll phone and ask him," but just then there was a knock on the door and her Dad came in!

"Something terrible has happened," he began. "I daren't tell you—" but the lady interrupted him to say that she knew because the medium had told her. He was really sorry and said, "The silly little sods were looking for mice. I just didn't see them." I stood up to leave and reassured the lady that her little cats were in the kitchen with her. Just then, the kettle started to boil without any of us touching it… The lady smiled at last and told me that one of the cats was always climbing onto the worktop and catching the kettle switch. Rather an unusual piece of evidence for survival, that.

Late one afternoon, a man rang to say that his two spaniels had gone missing; he lived on an isolated farm and asked if I knew where they were. I said I'd try to help and did a meditation that night, asking Spirit to help. I was shown a barn where some hay bales had fallen down, trapping the dogs and injuring them. I rang the man but he wouldn't believe me, saying he'd already looked there. I told him to look again and a few hours later he called to say I'd been right. One had a broken leg and the other was unconscious when they were found, but they were both at the vet's now. Two weeks later he sent me a letter to say that they were both doing well and enclosed another large cheque, which went straight to the animal sanctuary.

People do become very attached to their pets; they become part of the family. A lady contacted me for a reading concerning her 'furry baby', wanting to know if it was safe in Heaven with Grandma, so I used the Angel Cards for this reading because they are more specific and gentler than the Tarot. But this crafty lady and her partner had tried to trick me…

The first card told me that 'The pets are safe and well and are being looked after.' Plural? As I proceeded, I could smell the familiar Tea Tree shampoo that I use to bathe my own dogs with and then Spirit showed me two pink collars with little diamantes on them; I now knew that there were two dogs, not one as they had said. (Why people do this is beyond me.) I was shown a pink Wendy House with two little beds in it and a lot of toys. Finally, two little chinchillas came through to me themselves: they were identical except that one had an eye missing and the other one's eyes were a hazy blue, suggesting that they were both blind. I passed on all this to the couple along with describing an older spirit lady who was with the dogs.

The woman turned on her partner and said, "I told you it wasn't a good idea to lie, saying about only one of our babies. You've made us look like fools." Then she apologised to me. "I'm so sorry, we have been to so many psychics and no-one else picked up that there were two dogs. We just wanted to know that they are with Grandma." I told her I wasn't offended and assured them that their dogs were now healed and that they still visit their little Wendy House, so if they heard noises there it would be them.

"Would you ask them," she said, "if it's okay for us to get two more dogs?"

9

History Lessons

I was waiting at the doctor's surgery one day and picked up a local newspaper. Inside was a column written by a psychic medium who wrote that this was the last piece she was able to write for the paper. So when I got home I called the newspaper to see if they had replaced her; they hadn't and I asked if I could be considered for the job. I was asked to send in some examples of work I had done, for them to decide if I was suitable, so I sent my CV. Then I cut the psychic column out of the newspaper and made a request to Spirit that I wanted that column…

Five days later I was the newspaper's psychic columnist! I covered every spiritual subject possible, did questions and answers, and I predicted what would happen in the coming year. I loved this work and wrote for the newspaper for three years, also doing one-to-one readings – until fate took a hand again.

I believe that Spirit stops you when they can see you are taking on too much. I began to get very tired and nauseated, and investigations showed that I had kidney and liver failure due to all the pain medications. My husband wasn't well either. So I had to stop doing personal readings and writing for the newspaper; I was gutted, it felt just like when I had lost my nursing job, but I didn't have the energy to do anything. I was extremely down but I took it on board that I needed to rest.

We decided to spend more time at our caravan in Whitby, which we'd had for a long time. In fact, my husband had bought the caravan so that his Mam could have some holidays with us now that the kids were grown up and liked to go abroad but, sadly, she died from kidney failure one day before the site opened. We had watched the fireworks on New Year's Eve from her flat but when I put my arm around her I'd known that her time was limited. She had been an amazing mother-in-law and I loved her very much.

Well, after a few weeks of resting, I was getting bored. I had been reading a lot of history books and one day decided to visit Whitby Abbey, where I sat for a couple of hours just looking at the stained glass windows of St Mary's. A voice said, "You have work to do," but of course when I looked around there was no-one there. Still, I could feel my psychic energy returning. Then Spirit paid a visit to our caravan…

I could not believe what appeared in my bedroom there. Now, we had two dogs with us, my husband's Mollie and Paddy, my fox terrier, and I was reading in the early hours with Paddy lying at my side. I heard a low growl from him and looked up to see, hovering above me, a man with long black curly hair and a moustache. He was wearing a frilly white shirt covered with blood, a beautiful jacket with frilly cuffs and yellow fleur-de-lis on the front, black breeches with white tights and black shoes with buckles. His black eyes seemed to look right through me.

"They stabbed me in the back," he said, then vanished leaving a smell of eau de cologne.

My husband came out of his bedroom saying, "What is that awful smell? You shouldn't be spraying your perfume around this time of night." I told him I'd just seen a ghost but he laughed and thought I must have been dreaming. But no, I had seen the Cavalier clearly and wondered why he had shown himself to me.

He looked and dressed like a dandy in the time of Charles 1st but I am not a history expert so I tried to research the fleur-de-lis on his jacket, hoping to find some clue to his identity. This emblem was used as a design motif connected to the saints of France and the dress fashions of the 1620s seemed to fit my bloody Cavalier. But who was he?

I decided to research the area of our caravan site, at Ugthorpe Lodge. The hotel there was used as a hunting lodge for people calling in for refreshments on their way up to the north of Yorkshire. But I could find no mention of any fighting here so I was baffled by why a Cavalier would come through to me in my caravan. He was obviously an Earthbound ghost, a wandering spirit who couldn't go to the light, so were there any other reports of hauntings around here?

The actual hotel is supposed to be haunted by two children so I thought I would visit and see what I experienced. As I was coming out of one room something caught my eye, a woman wearing a grey dress and carrying a lamp. It was for only a second but I could smell the oil of the lamp as she brushed past me. I also heard children giggling on the stairs but didn't see them. On the field nearby, where I take the dogs walking, I have seen occasionally what looks like a priest. He is too far away for me to see his face and when I get closer to him he vanishes.

"Oh, that's Father Postgate," said the site owner, "he often comes onto the site." I researched him and found that a Father Nicholas was a seventeenth century Catholic priest who was executed – hung, drawn and quartered – for hiding priests from France.

Perhaps it's strange, but I like to see ghosts and there are plenty in the north of Yorkshire. One of my local heroines is St Hilda, or Abbess Hild of Whitby, who built a monastery on the East Cliff in 657 and was famous for her wisdom. Several kings sought her out and St Edwin, King of Northumbria, is buried there. Hild loved Whitby Abbey but because of poor health moved to Hackness where she had founded another monastery;

she was buried there and one of her nuns, Begu, reported seeing her soul rise up to Heaven escorted by a band of angels. This location seemed promising…

I sat looking towards the Abbey one cold day, hoping to catch a glimpse of something (I was also writing a feature on Whitby for a magazine at the time), and focused on my surroundings to see what I could pick up. The graveyard across from where I sat did seem to have a lot of spiritual energy during the two hours I watched, but there was no sign of St Hilda or any nuns. So I got up to go into St Mary's church for a cup of tea and to get warm.

Just then I saw a white mist and little orbs hovering over one of the graves. I looked around but there was no-one about – the graveyard was in disrepair and clearly not visited often, which seems disrespectful to me – so I walked over to the grave with the mist over it and looked down. The inscription read, 'Here lies John Brown, Master Mariner'. The mist vanished.

"We drowned. It was not my fault," said a gruff voice. He didn't appear, though, I only heard the voice. 'Oh well,' I thought, 'some spiritual activity if not quite what I was hoping for.' There are many other stories of hauntings in the area, including St Hilda's Church at Egton, five miles to the west, which is said to be haunted by a donkey, though I haven't been donkey-hunting yet.

I love castles so one time when we were at our caravan in Whitby we decided to go to Bamburgh Castle in Northumberland. It was greatly restored and modernised in late-Victorian times but there have been settlements on the site since prehistoric days. It looks majestic now but I was sure there must be plenty of ghosts there and I wanted to see them. In fact, the first room I walked into was buzzing with Spirit activity and I was glad I'd protected myself before going in.

A little spirit maid was on her knees, sweeping dust into a pan; she wore a frilly hat but when I looked again she had vanished. There were orbs of light darting everywhere about the room. A lot of visitors come here so I had to remind myself not to start talking to the ghosts! In the third room I entered was a spirit man in front of me who looked perhaps like a gamekeeper, wearing a deerstalker hat. He was looking angrily at all the people walking around and touching things and he shouted at me, "Get out of my home!" In my research later I recognised him as Lord Armstrong, the famous industrialist who had restored the castle.

As we walked down the steps to the dungeons, both my husband and I heard a high-pitched scream and the cry of a baby, but there was no-one about, only us. When we got to the bottom of the steps I looked into a jail cell and saw sitting there a young lad with a dead pheasant on his knee and blood dripping down his leg. He looked at me and said, "I was flogged for stealing." Having seen my ghosts I was getting very tired so I sat down on one of the benches; someone squeezed my arm but I couldn't see who it was. We took several photographs while we were there and when we looked at them later they all had little orb faces on them.

Even though my husband is totally uninterested in my spiritual side, we have both always been fascinated by WWI (I believe my husband's guide is a soldier from that time). I shed a tear when I read about how those brave men fought for king and country, miles from home and away from their loved ones. One year we booked a tour to Belgium to see the battlefields.

Before we left, I did a meditation and asked whether any First World War spirits would like to come forward, and a slight, dark-haired young man in uniform, aged around twenty, appeared bringing the smell of gunpowder. He gave his name as Jack and when I asked him what it was like fighting then he replied grimly, "Hell on Earth." He waved an arm and showed me a field pitted with craters and muddy trenches and strewn with the dead and barbed wire. Then he showed me a dead horse and started to cry. I could hear shouts of pain and could smell the white lily scent of death. I thought, 'This is going to be some tour.'

The day after arriving in Belgium we went to the Essex Farm military cemetery, just north of Ypres, and I knew I was in for a bumpy ride – I could already smell the white lilies. This had been a strategic position during the war, standing in the way of

Germany's advance across western Europe. At the cemetery, there were some Army dug-outs where wounded soldiers were brought for treatment by doctors and I felt drawn towards them. I could smell the blood and saw horribly injured soldiers, as the spirit of a thin, exhausted-looking doctor in a blood-stained apron rushed past me. He had red hair and spoke with some kind of accent as he shouted that he needed more room to work. Someone called back, "We'll try, Mac!" I stood mesmerised as the red-haired man passed me and looked directly at me; I will never forgot that haunting gaze.

I headed out of the bunkers to join my husband, and promptly fell over a memorial stone. The inscription commemorated Lieutenant Colonel John McCrae, a Canadian poet, soldier and doctor who had worked as a surgeon here in Ypres. He is also famous for his poem In Flanders Fields. Was this the spirit in my vision? When I got back from Belgium, I researched John McCrae and gasped when I saw his photograph on the screen: he was the man covered in blood in the dugout that I had seen. The words of his beautiful poem came to my mind:

> *To you from falling hands we throw*
> *the torch; be yours to hold up high.*
> *If ye break faith with us who die,*
> *we shall not sleep,*
> *though poppies grow in Flanders fields.*

I felt glad that I had done what I could to hold that torch and to remember the war in which so many brave men had fought and died. They will not let me forget, and nor should any of us.

There was still more to see and more spirits to find me. On the next day of our tour we were taken to Vimy Ridge in northern France. Today, a huge memorial stands there as a testimony to the Canadian First Army Corps who fought so bravely in 1917, helping the Allies to win the war. The ground beneath is honeycombed with tunnels where the soldiers lived, and when we came to the Communications Room there I felt a blast of cold wind. The spirit of a short youth clutching a metal canister appeared, looked at me and said, "I am Ronny Runner," then sped off. 'Runner' was obviously his job description and he was on his way to deliver a message to some military officials along one of the many tunnels, possibly having to travel at least ten miles.

I was contacted later by a lady from Ireland who had read a magazine feature I had written on this subject. She explained that her Great Uncle Jonny had joined the Army as a young man and had gone to fight in Belgium, but she did not know how or where he died. Please would I do a meditation and try to bring him forward? She sent me a photograph of Jonny looking very young. I said I would try to help, but I cannot predict who will come through – I can only ask and all I had to go on was a photo.

I waited until all my family were out so I wouldn't be disturbed (there's nothing worse than calling a spirit forward and then someone shouts, "Do you want a cup of tea?"). From mid-afternoon I waited and waited until it was getting dark and the family would soon be home, feeling very disappointed that I had failed. But I'm like a dog with a bone when I set out to do something so I was determined to try again… Next day, I suggested to my husband that he went fishing for the day and off he went happily with a flask of tea and sandwiches.

Jonny came through after about thirty minutes. He told me he had been blown up at Poperinge, near Ypres, and his limbs were scattered in a muddy field. He became very tearful and explained, "We never had a chance. We were like pigs to the slaughter. There was a flash and we were gone. Jimmy and Tom died too." Then he added, "But I've got my body back – I am whole and with Mum and Dad." His relative come over to England to thank me and took me out for a nice meal at the hotel where she and her friend were staying; later they visited the field where Great Uncle Jonny had died and laid a wreath of poppies.

On another visit to the battlefields, it was nearly the end of the week when we went to a city called Arras in France where there had been a great battle on the Western Front. It is a charming place with narrow cobbled streets but the war damage was still evident. I had a bad back so went to sit on a bench in a churchyard. I was just admiring the view when someone came to sit beside me and I turned round to see a nun – she had a hole in her chest! She was only there a minute and then vanished. I couldn't stop thinking about her so decided to go into the church and make enquires, hoping to find some pictures. All the pews were empty except one where a nun was sitting so I walked down the aisle to where she was; it was the same nun who had sat with me outside. It is very unusual to see the same ghost in two different places. She faced me and said, "Shot dead. Resistance. Sister Marie saved soldiers." When I got home, I did some research to try and find a nun who had been in the Resistance but I haven't been able to identify the woman I saw.

By now, I was getting stronger mentally and wanted to do more with my gift. For example, when I went to the supermarket I would see people's auras and sometimes a spirit attached nearby but I felt it could be embarrassing to approach those individuals. On the other hand, I was getting a lot of requests for personal readings and was happy to do about four of these each day.

It was during one of these readings that a geisha girl came through for the first time. I had told my client about her spirit guide, a Victorian lady who had fallen down some steps in her home and died, when Mateo Oso appeared in front of me and said, "I am your guide." At first I ignored her because for one thing I was doing a reading for my client and also because I knew that Black Feather was my guide. I finished the reading and my next client was waiting so I put Mateo Oso to the back of my mind.

After I had finished, I called at the chip shop for our tea and on the way back there was a strong smell of lilac. 'Who wears lilac perfume these days?' I thought, turning round to look. Whoosh,

Mateo Oso was beside me. I just smiled at her and then she vanished, but I knew I would see her again. She came through later in a dream, showing me that her hands and feet were bandaged (this was traditional). Then I saw a vision of her arms with no hands; she showed me a necklace of emeralds and said, "I borrowed them and they chopped my hands off." Since then she has come to me often, especially when I am doing my craft work: if I cannot decide which fabric to use, a piece will fall on the floor or I will hear her voice in my head, along with the fragrance of lilacs.

My spiritual energy was becoming very strong again and I started to visit people at their homes to do readings. This was helpful because when I walked into a person's home I could feel the energy there and see the client's aura very clearly. One day, I had a phone call from a man who said, "Is that the psychic who sees things? I think my daughter is going funny, she says she see things." Well, of course that rang a very loud bell in my head and brought back the memory of when I was a girl and my Grandma Mac had said, "Don't tell folk that you see things because they'll think you've gone funny in the head." The man asked how much I would charge and I replied that it would be nothing, because it concerned his daughter. He didn't believe me at first but then gave me his address and I agreed to go the next day; I was determined to make time to see this girl even though I was very busy.

I assembled my tools, a sage stick, my pendulum and black tourmaline, turquoise and rose quartz crystals. As soon as I walked into the house I could smell burning but this wasn't the wood smoke that Black Feather gives, it was awful, like burnt flesh. The little girl was sat at the kitchen table looking very frightened, sad and dejected.

"Hello," I said, "your Dad is a bit worried about you." Straight off, she told me that her Mum had left because of her husband's drinking; I had already seen that the bin was full of beer cans but that was not my concern, it was the little girl who was my priority. I told her there were certain things I could do to help her but there was nothing to be frightened of, and described how

103

when I had been her age I'd begun to see things, like the colours of the aura around people; I had seen spirits and I knew things that no-one else did, but I'd been warned not to say anything because I might be locked up.

"Can you see the things that I see?" she asked. I hadn't told her yet that I could see a young girl sitting at the table beside her in a wispy green dress who had burns on her arm and smelled of burning. So first I asked her to tell me what she had been seeing. "I was in the kitchen getting our tea ready," she said, "when some-one poked me in the back and I could smell burning. I just saw the colour green and then it vanished." I glanced at the spirit girl who was looking at me and saying, "I fell into the fire." The girl then said she had felt someone hugging her and also that when she had gone to the bathroom at school to wash her hands there had been a face staring back at her in the mirror.

"There's nothing wrong with you," I said, "and I know who it is haunting you. It's a little girl who fell into a fire – but she only wants to be your friend." "A ghost wants to be my friend?" she said. "People will think I've gone crackers if I tell them that." I told her that I could help the spirit girl go to the light so she would not be bothered again, if that's what she wanted. First, she looked around the kitchen, scattered with beer bottles, and it was clear that it was her parents who worried her most. "Will my Mum come back?" she asked. "She ran off with my Dad's best friend. It destroyed my Dad, as you can see from state of house." I had to say that I didn't think her parents would get back together, and that her father needed her more. Then she said, "Please do send the girl to the light," so I did that.

Later, I had a conversation with her Dad and told him that, yes, his daughter could 'see things' but that I had now cleansed their house; moreover, he needed to help the girl by cutting down the drinking and getting the house tidied up. I knew a lovely lady who could help. Before I left, I gave the girl my crystals – tourmaline for grounding, turquoise to dispel negativity and rose quartz for new love – and said that whenever she felt sad and needed help she could give me a call, which she did for some time afterwards. I was the first to know that her Dad was now in a happy relationship with the cleaning lady I had told him about! The girl later went to university and got a professional job, and she tells me that she's now in touch with her spiritual side thanks to what we shared.

10

Crystals, Dreams, Leaves and Cards

Earlier, I wrote about using a pendulum to help us answer troublesome questions, and here I'd like to describe some of the other spiritual 'tools' and methods that have been helpful to me, hoping that this inspires you in your own psychic development!

By now, I was doing regular personal readings as well as submitting articles for magazines on a range of spiritual subjects. The only trouble with the writing was that my column was christened Our Psychic Nurse Glynis so I would get some very odd enquiries… For example, "I have to visit the loo every time I go out and it's so embarrassing. What do you advise?" Naturally, my answer was that there could be an underlying problem such as an infection or prolapsed bladder, so the reader needed to see their doctor. On the other hand, I could offer spiritual help too: an aquamarine crystal can help to balance fluids in the body, whilst jade and mookaite (an Australian jasper) are also good for urinary incontinence.

Of course, a common request was whether there is a crystal that can help to attract money. Yes, there is. If you keep orange carnelian and yellow citrine in your purse it will never be empty. I do this myself because I really believe in crystals and their properties. For example, I wear an amethyst 'super seven' crystal made up of seven different compounds and also a tiger's eye for protection and luck. (Roman soldiers wore both these crystals when they went to war.) Crystals have a magic all of their own and sometimes, when I need an answer, instead of using the pendulum I go to my crystal box and pick out two at random – they always tell me what I want to know.

The two crystals that I probably use, and advise clients to use, more than others are rose quartz, which attracts love and helps us to forgive mistakes (including our own), and turquoise, which calms the mind and protects against 'bad entities' or dark thoughts. But some of my magazine readers' questions were definitely not spiritual… One man asked me if I could (psychically?) cure his sore throat because he was a public speaker; he admitted to drinking whisky every day, having a 'dicky liver' and sometimes spitting blood. Well, I could only advise him to see a doctor urgently (I thought he might have an underlying throat condition such as oesophageal varices, which often occurs with people who have an alcohol problem). There are no crystals that could have helped him.

Many ancient cultures believed that dreams enable supernatural communication, because our rational minds are resting and Spirit can pass through the veil between worlds. Science has never been able to explain why we dream although for a long time the most common theory was that of the father of psychoanalysis, Sigmund Freud. His interpretation was that dreams represent a disguised fulfilment of our repressed desires. Carl Jung also famously believed that studying dreams is a means to understanding the unconscious psychology of the mind.

Nowadays, many people have moved on from such theories and are open to the idea that extra-sensory perception (ESP) can be at work in our dreams, for example clairvoyance and precognition. In my experience, we can even make contact with the spirit world and receive messages from our guides, relatives or angels. Perhaps the most famous such dream is described in the Biblical Book of Genesis (Chapter 28): fleeing from his powerful brother Esau, Jacob dreamed of a ladder leading up to Heaven on which angels were going up and down. Then 'God' stood next to him – was this a spirit guide? – and reassured him about his spiritual path and destiny.

I always keep a note of dream messages and have often had clear dreams of the future that have come true. In particular, I find that the colours in dreams are very revealing.

Gold	Dreaming of something with a golden colour means that you will find some kind of great treasure or that your spirituality will be heightened. You may see the Archangel Jophiel, the angel of 'the Golden Flame', who wears a golden dress. If she is watching over you then you are blessed.
Silver	Silver in a dream suggests that you have greater power than perhaps you believe. You can stand alone and have an almost magical influence over people. Every problem has 'a silver lining' and you can solve it.
Purple	This represents spirituality – perhaps you can develop psychic gifts or become a spiritual healer.
White	This colour signifies purity of heart, a sign that your higher self is becoming more spiritual. It is also the colour of approaching abundance.
Black	This is not what you might expect; it tells you that you have the power to do anything you want (within reason!) when you use your intuition and act with dignity.

Red	This colour represents great strength and the ability to confront danger head on. But it can also reveal hidden temper and passion, depending on other details.
Pink	A clear message that you are entering a new period of romance and a warm, loving atmosphere. Pink is related to the heart chakra so there will be plenty of love to receive – and to give back.
Yellow	This is the colour of intelligence, but it can suggest that sometimes you are afraid to act on your thoughts for fear of the consequences.
Green	A colour that represents abundance and good fortune (perhaps benefiting from someone's generosity); it is also linked to healing abilities.
Blue	You are protected by Spirit. The colour also signifies honesty, wisdom and inspiration.
Brown	The colour of Mother Earth. Your life will be fruitful but you may need a rest from your many commitments.
Orange	A zesty colour representing enthusiasm for life. It can suggest a renewal of interest, and success, in an academic subject too.
Grey	Unsurprisingly, a grey dream represents confusion about something – you need guidance to know which way to go.

There are many books and Internet sites that offer help with interpreting dream symbolism but sometimes you are the only one who can intuitively know what certain things are trying to tell you. Here are just a few archetypal images that often turn up in spiritual dreams:

Abbey	This or a similar religious building means that your difficulties are coming to an end.

Baby	Yes, it could foretell a pregnancy but usually you are being warned to prepare for a death of someone (or something).
Eyes	The eyes are windows to the soul so you will soon see things you did not think possible or something important to your higher self.
Falcon	This or other birds of prey can signify an increase in status or wealth, but can also be a warning about enemies nearby!
Grass	Watch out for deceptive situations or people (it isn't 'greener on the other side').
Hat	Wearing one is a sure sign of success in a new venture.
Kite	Success again ('flying high') or a prediction of a journey.
Lake	Water always represents our emotions so how does it appear? If it's rough then expect trouble but all will be well if it's calm.
Path	This is straightforward – if the way is clear then you're going the right way, but a crooked or rough path usually predicts ill-health.
Scissors	A relationship is coming to an end. On a spiritual level, you are being advised to try and let go of past hurts.
Veil	To see someone wearing a veil suggests that things are being hidden from you. But a black veil is a harbinger of death (of someone or something).
Warts	This is a strange symbol – this or similar skin blemishes nearly always predicts wealth!

This is just a taste of the weird and wonderful symbolic language of dreams. It's possible to train yourself to remember your dreams, by setting that intention for your mind when you go to bed. When you wake up, use your phone's voice recorder to make a note of what you've seen or heard, and find a comprehensive book of dream symbols to help you interpret things. After a while, your own intuition will develop and meanings will become clearer in your mind.

For example, I was distraught when my fox terrier Paddy died suddenly and was afraid that perhaps he'd choked on something I'd given him or that he'd picked up something on our walk. But then I dreamed that I saw him at the Rainbow Bridge with my other animals and on his head was a heart symbol with something like raindrops on it. This helped to reassure me and it was confirmed later that he'd had a leaking heart valve that led to a heart attack.

Occasionally, dreams will be perfectly clear. One September day I had an unsettled feeling all day and kept seeing aeroplanes and smoke in my mind without knowing why. This was a kind of 'waking dream' – they don't always come in the night. Eventually, I put the TV on and realised why my mind had been so disturbed, as I watched the 9/11 Twin Towers disaster unfold with aeroplanes smashing into the American sky scrapers. For a long time, I couldn't stop thinking about those people and how frightened they must have been and even now I light a candle every year on the anniversary.

I was invited by a heart charity to contribute to a psychic event by reading the tea leaves. This was fine with me (and I have a red spotted tea set that I always use) although I knew that Spirit sometimes gives me messages for the client at the same time. There were lots of other psychics doing their bit for charity at the event although I had the longest queue! Nearby sat a man offering crystal ball readings who looked quite dejected because he had hardly any clients and I felt a bit sorry for him.

"Can you read the tea leaves?" I asked him.

"Never tried," he answered. "But I am a psychic so I'll give it a go." I passed over a cup and my teapot with loose tea in it and gave him my next client. I heard what he then said to the lady and she was beaming, very satisfied. It just goes to show that almost anyone can learn to do it, with some knowledge and some psychic ability. After the lady had left, he thanked me and said, "Not many people would have done that." Well, I had been in the same position in the past, with people walking past me and going to the well-known psychics (even though I knew I was just as good as them!).

I always tell my clients that I never know what is going to be in the cup, so are they happy to take what comes? The leaves can be very clear – sometimes I am shown things that are definitely not very nice – and we have to be careful how we deliver the news. One client at this event was a very nervous lady who kept looking around her and said she had just had her palm read by another psychic who had told her "some horrible stuff." I said we'd do her reading and then she could tell me all about it, so I poured her tea and connected to Spirit while she drank it.

The first image I saw was of a building with bars on it, then there were two figures laid flat, side by side. There was also a car with a light on top and a long box that resembled a coffin. I relayed all this to the lady and her tears started to flow. She told me that her son had been in a fight with someone who had fallen and hit his head on the pavement and subsequently died. Her boy was now looking at a murder charge and a long prison sentence. The reading verified that he would indeed go to prison (and the car with a light must have represented the police). Yet also in the cup were images of a pram and a baby – the lady confirmed that her son's girlfriend was having a baby. Like I said, the tea leaves can be very clear and this reading made me feel so sad. Still, the lady asked for my card to keep in touch and a year later she came to see me, bringing along her little grandson. Her son had received a sentence of twelve years in prison for manslaughter.

The spiritual 'tools' I have mentioned – such as the pendulum, crystals and tea leaves – don't contain messages themselves, they are all ways of nudging the unconscious mind to reach out for information psychically. Another similar method used by many mediums, and which I learned for myself, is reading Tarot Cards. I have several clients who come for these readings time and time again (though I ask that they wait four months inbetween) and there's one lady I really love to see because she always brings me a gift of shower gel!

One day she walked into the room with a murky grey aura and I thought something awful must have happened to her. We sat ourselves down and she chose her cards, but she was very quiet which wasn't like her at all. When I asked if she was okay she just shook her head. So I started to read the cards but, as each one came out, the story was getting worse and worse...

While I was reading the cards, a spirit man came through to me too. He had an aura of green haze and red around his head, symbolising both anger and healing, and he had red marks on his neck. I told my client that this angry man was here and that he'd been very determined to get through and give her a message.

"Go on then," she said with resignation, "let's hear it."

"I did not do what they say I did," was his message. "There's no reason for me to lie because I am here now." (He meant, in the spirit world.)

"Then why the hell did you hang yourself?" she asked him, which came as a bit of a shock to me. "It's like proving you're guilty."

I could feel the atmosphere becoming very tense and the spirit man was very upset because it seemed that she didn't believe him.

Then he was gone and she just shook her head. After a while, she told me the story: the man was her ex-partner who'd been accused of being a paedophile – he couldn't cope with what everyone was saying about him so he had hung himself. However, for the first time ever, Black Feather now stepped into an actual reading and clearly said to me, "He is innocent." I told the lady this and added that my own feeling was also that he was innocent.

"We shall see," she said quietly. "The investigations are still going on at the moment."

It turned out that this poor man had been blamed – and framed – for an horrendous crime he did not commit and had been so distraught that he took his own life. When the police investigation finished, it concluded that he was indeed not guilty – but it was too late for him. Another man, a drug addict, had blamed him for abusing his daughter when in fact it was the girl's father himself. How cruel.

On the other hand, this Tarot reading was an example of how accurate and helpful the cards can be. This was the layout that my client had drawn from the Major Arcana, along with my comments:

The Devil	There is a mischief-maker who shifts blame onto other people. He or she is a liar and preys on gullible people but will be caught out one day soon.
Judgement	Like a phoenix rising from the ashes, you and those you love will triumph when the truth is revealed. It will be too late for someone but they can be helped by others standing up for them. Act on the information received and hold your head up high for there is no stigma. This person is innocent.
The Hierophant	Listen to your inner voice to know the way ahead. The truth will come out and then there will be sorrowful thoughts and changes in people's lives.

115

Temperance	Wisdom and restraint are needed. The guilty will be caught out and the innocent will be exonerated. Then it will be time to move on from bad times. Those who have been hurt will be healed by angels and soon things will be settled.
The Emperor	Reclaim your life and go with the changes. A visit to the doctor is indicated – panic attacks? This strong card can also mean the law is involved.
The World	Your world is now in your hands and you can move on with whatever you want to do, knowing that the slate is clean.
The Lovers	This card at the end rather surprised me, symbolising a new loving relationship coming into the lady's life, someone connected to her ex-partner. I was sure, though, that it represented a long and happy life together.

She then told me that she'd been separated from the man in spirit for quite a while before the incident happened, and actually she was now seeing his brother. (They did eventually get married.) So despite what everybody had been thinking, the Tarot had clearly given the truth and urged my client to stand up for it and to move forward.

But that wasn't the end of the matter. The lady came back to me six months later and so did the spirit man – with a vengeance!

"I told you I was innocent and that I was framed," he said, "but you didn't believe me." She started to cry. 'Good grief,' I thought, 'no-one would believe this – we're having a full-scale domestic row between a woman and a spirit!' "Crocodile tears," he added.

"What was I to think," she replied, very upset now and almost shouting at the man (whom she couldn't see, of course), "when everyone was talking about you as a paedophile and the police took you away?"

I thought I'd better stop this now because it was getting out of hand, so I said to the man, "I let you come through to me with all good intentions. Now, a big mistake was made but it wasn't this lady's fault and she is very sorry that you lost your life." With that he murmured, "Sorry" and vanished. After this, I blocked him and carried on with the reading.

The lady later left me with a pink, loving aura. I gave her a rose quartz crystal to help with the forgiveness of mistakes and to strengthen the love in her life. I suggested that she put the crystal in a quiet place with two pink, lighted candles, and ask Venus, the angel of love, to come forward and bring her peace. Placing a photo of her new lover with the crystal would also protect the relationship. I also gave her a turquoise crystal, to calm her mind.

Angel Cards have become very popular with many people now-adays and I will also sometimes use them in a reading if I feel they're particularly appropriate. Now, I normally only do readings for people over sixteen years of age but one of my regular clients asked me to see a young, very streetwise girl of fifteen whose mother, my client's friend, had died tragically. The girl's Mum had died from a drugs overdose and her daughter had found her body. I could hardly imagine the sadness and trauma of this.

As they walked into my room, a spirit woman who looked no more than about thirty years old came with them. I thought this couldn't be the girl's mother because she was too young but my client told me, when I asked, that her friend had had her daughter at fourteen. My heart went out to this young girl: both her Mum and Dad were gone, now she lived with her very strict grandmother and they did not get on together. My strong intu-ition was that the Angel Cards would be the most helpful with this situation and I told the girl we'd use these to communicate with her Mum.

"Oh, we've already tried that with my friend's Ouija Board," she said, very cocky. I told her how dangerous that can be and that she might attract bad forces that could make her ill (remembering my own past experiences). "I don't care," she said. "I just want to talk to my Mum." Well, at least no dark entities had come with her. She shuffled the cards, picked out five, and the reading went like this:

Adriana	You are being led towards the answer to your prayers, so please listen carefully and follow the advice given. Your Mum is talking to you through your intuition and your thoughts and dreams. The girl said that, yes, her Mum had come into her dreams. "She says she loves me and she's sorry for leaving me." I reassured her that her Mum was with her all the time.
Archangel Uriel	Your emotions are beginning to heal and you will become open to love again. This angel helps to release anger and blame from your heart and mind. But the girl shouted, "I don't believe in angels – they took my Mum away from me." This was tough, the poor girl was so confused and angry. Now, I rarely call upon Mateo Oso but this time I silently asked her to come forward with her gentle nature and beautiful fragrance of lilac, to give this child some comforting love. Straight away, the girl asked, "What's that smell?" but I kept quiet.
Sonya	This angel brings you a message from your loved one in Spirit. She says, "I am at peace and I love you very much. Please don't worry about me." I took the girl's hand and silently asked Archangel Raphael to come forward and give her some healing, and I could feel the energy running through my hands to hers.

She pulled back and said, "I felt something strange then, like being overwhelmed with love." I told her that this was her Mum, bringing her love and healing with an angel's help, and she asked me which angel it was. We were making progress now, the girl's mother and the angels were getting through to her. I told her that she could call on Raphael at any time when she was feeling unhappy.

Shanti The angel of peace brings you new tranquility and a smoother road ahead. She replied, "I love that name. Is she really an angel and please can I have that card?" I said that of course she could, in fact she could have the whole pack; no child should go through the turmoil she'd had and if giving her my Angel Cards helped her then that was okay with me.

The cards needed cleansing because they had my energy all over them so I gave the lady who'd brought her my sage stick and told her how to do that outside while I carried on with the reading.

Zanna You are protected from all types of harm. No matter what has happened in the past, your future is assured and you are protected by the angels. They will help to heal your heart. "You chose these cards, not me," I said to her finally, "so take notice of what they are saying to you."

She began to tell me some of her story, for example of when she'd been taken to a drugs den where one of the men had offered her Mum money to 'have a good time' with her daughter. Her Mum was out of her head. The situation had got really bad after the girl's father died; the mother had gone downhill, got in with some drug dealers and then spent all her money on drugs. The girl's grandmother had disowned them both.

"Coming here to see you today has changed my outlook on life," she said. "I'll try to get on with my grandmother and make her proud of me."

"What's done is done and can't be altered," I replied, "but you must have forgiveness in your heart. Just keep the good memories of your Mum and Dad and know that they loved you very much." In fact, her mother was standing right beside her but I felt I couldn't tell her because it might frighten her. But she said, "I can feel my Mum is here."

She didn't look at all scared, actually quite at peace so now I told her that her mother had been with us all along, telling me all about her. "You are wearing her cross and chain," I said, and the girl opened her coat to show me. "I shall never forget you," she said. "I never thought I would be able to move forward but you've made that happen."

There would be one last card to end the reading:

Celeste   There will be a happy move to a new home and this will bring in a new, positive energy. This 'new home' would be a new start at her grandmother's, where she would be loved and supported.

I ended by telling the girl that her mother would never be far away, that she would guide her throughout her life, so she should talk with her in her mind. When she was feeling more settled, her Mum would give signs to reassure her daughter that she was nearby. The happy outcome to the story is that this girl is now married with two children and works as a nurse in a Drug Addiction Unit.

Oh yes, and she sent me a new deck of Angel Cards!

11

This Job Can Be Tough!

Occasionally, I will get a really awkward client who questions everything so much that it's almost impossible to get on with the reading. I always make sure that I'm well protected, both physically and spiritually, but sometimes I need more!

One particular day I had a phone call from a lady in her fifties who wanted to come with her husband. This made me feel uneasy all day because I don't usually read for couples together, afraid that I might blurt out something I shouldn't, something embarrassing. Well, they pulled up outside my house in a very expensive car and I could see immediately that the man had been drinking. 'This is going to be tough going,' I thought, so I put extra protection around myself and asked Archangel Michael, the warrior protector, to come forward. Then I did a quick 'bubble protection' as the couple came in. For this, I imagine a bubble of pure white light that I step into, then visualise a heavy purple cloak covering my body. I was also wearing my usual turquoise and black tourmaline protective crystals. Sometimes, it's a wonder that any spirits can get through all my protection and come forward…

121

The man began by wanting to know why I use crystals, what was that smell (Nag Champa incense), how long had I been a psychic, was I registered and why did I charge money for readings? I replied that I wanted to carry on living so I had expenses to pay, but I give half the fees to kidney disease research, which shut him up temporarily. The lady looked very embarrassed and sat looking at the floor, probably hoping that it would swallow her up – or him. At last the man said that he'd brought his wife here because he believed that she'd been unfaithful and he wanted me to tell him the truth. After all, she was very beautiful and much younger than him.

I did not like this at all but decided to go ahead with a card reading while I also silently asked for any spirits connected to this couple to come forward. They did – but they were not who I expected. It was the man's mother along with a younger-looking man who looked very much like the man sitting in my room. When I told the couple this, the husband clapped his hands and smirked.

"Ha! Caught you out. My mother is still alive and she only had me." Of all the clients I have seen, this was one of the most awkward and he was trying to catch me out. But I have faith in Spirit and they never let me down, so I continued with the spirit woman's message: "She really is your mother and she wants to say 'Sorry' to you. You had a twin brother who died in mysterious circumstances and you were taken away from her and adopted."

He sat open-mouthed for a moment then stood up and said, "I've heard enough. Come on, you, we'll go and find a genuine psychic." He picked up the CD recording, emptied my bag of crystals across the table and walked out (without paying). But that wasn't the end of it. A couple of days later, the wife came back to see me. Her husband had complained to his mother about the fake psychic who talked a load of rubbish about a twin brother… She had sat him down and told him that, yes, he was adopted; his twin brother had died in a fire caused by a cigarette and Social Services had taken the other boy away from his mother.

"You should have seen his face," said his wife, opening her purse and giving me double what I normally charge. "And he apologises for being so rude. Oh, and by the way, you got me out of a tight spot because I was having an affair. I've told him now and packed my bags." I still wonder how I would have coped if the original reading had gone ahead as the man intended, because I have a code of ethics that means never betraying confidences. (A man once offered me hundreds of pounds to tell him what was in his wife's reading!)

But I do get to hear some shocking things. A very well-spoken and well-dressed lady came to see me and I had just started the reading – about normal things like a change of job and a new granddaughter – when a spirit woman came forward and said she was the lady's mother. She said to me that her daughter ought to keep her knickers on instead of dropping them for every man she sees… I told the lady that her Mum was here and saying something very personal.

"All right, what did the old bat say?" she said, so I relayed the message, keeping a straight face. My client retorted, "Mother, I have a husband and three boyfriends to keep happy!" She turned to me and went on, "Take no notice of her, she's just jealous." It beggars belief what I hear at times – and this lady looked so stern and upright too.

A young couple came to see me, distraught because they had lost their only child, and even though as I've said I don't usually read for couples this seemed very important. They both had dark grey auras, the lady's with some small areas of pink but no other colour, and their grief was weighing me down. I decided to use the Angel Cards and they agreed; as they chose the cards I could see that they were counting, so they had significant numbers in mind.

Merlina   This card showed that they were confused because they didn't have enough information; they needed to get advice before making some kind of decision. Spirit was telling me that their little girl died suddenly, wearing a red and white spotted dress and that she had spina bifida. They confirmed all this was true.

Yet I could also feel that this couple felt guilty about how it had happened. Spirit showed me a shunt coming out of the child's head (this drains excess fluid in the brain), and I knew that it had come out with no-one noticing because the child always wore a bonnet. When I reported this, the woman fainted. I gave her some smelling salts which I always keep handy and she said, "How could you possibly have known that?"

I said that Spirit had told me – and also that the couple wanted to try for another baby. Again they agreed this was true but said they were worried in case another child was disabled. So this is the decision that they needed medical advice on.

Isabella   The time is right for a new venture and a happy outcome will follow. This was the answer to their question: they had learned how to cope and were ready to be parents again.

"I have a lady here," I said, "with a scar on her face. Your little girl is with this lady and wearing her red spotted dress." The husband said that this lady was his mother and that they'd buried their child in that dress because it was her favourite.

Opal   This angel brought a message from their daughter, that she was in Heaven, that she was happy and being cared for by the angels. Her mother's smile was so beautiful to see. "I will never get over losing her," she said, "but I feel happier now, knowing that she is looked after by the angels and that it wasn't our fault."

A spirit man then came forward and said, "I'm her grandfather. It was an accident and the child had no chance to survive. She was very ill." They both began to cry now. After a while, the lady said again that they would try for another baby and I had to point out that the angels knew that already. "Look at the second card that came out," I said, "and, remember, you chose the cards, not me." Now they told me that they had used their girl's date of birth numbers in choosing which cards to pick!

The final card confirmed everything and surprised us all, even me.

Serephina   "There is some good news for you," I said. "Serephina is the angel of families and a happy addition is coming to your family. The angels have heard you, they have let you go through a period of adjustment and now you are ready. Actually… congratulations! I believe you're pregnant now." The grey aura gone, my client had certainly started to look 'blooming'. The lady with the scar came forward and said, "She is having a little boy." And she did, eight months later! What had started out as one of the most agonising of readings had ended in joy after all.

Another very sad lady came to see me, dressed in black from head to toe and very tearful when she arrived. She said, "My life has ended." We had a chat about what kind of reading she wanted and she chose the Angel Cards because she wanted angelic support. I was halfway through the reading when she suddenly pulled out a photo of a man.

"This is my son," she said. "He was very handsome and had the thickest black hair I've ever seen." I then told her that when she had come into my home there was a spirit man walking in with her but he was bald. "That's my son," she said. "I know you're genuine now. I've been to so many mediums and you're the only one who picked up that, yes, my son was bald." The man then moved to his mother's side and I heard the sound of a train and then screaming and shouting, which told me that he had been killed in an accident with a train. "That's right," she replied. "He shouldn't have been on that track – the trains hadn't been diverted."

The spirit man sat beside his mother nodding his head at this, then gave me one of the strangest messages I've ever heard. "Tell her I know what she was doing and I appreciate it, but it's too late now. She cut all the family's hair and made it into a wig for me—" He laughed loudly. "I would never have worn it but don't tell her that!" I passed on what he wanted me to say and she became much happier than when she'd arrived, knowing that her son had made contact and was safe and well.

"I know for sure that it is my son who has come through to you," she said, "because no-one else knew about that."

Some of these stories have touched me personally much more than others. Near my home one day, I saw a lady struggling with a Zimmer frame as she tried to take her little dog for a walk so I ran over and told her that I lived around the corner and could take her dog for walks with my dogs. She asked me to come to her flat for a chat afterwards.

After that, I saw Wynn every day and took Robbie for a walk. He would lie on her settee all day, never doing anything and looking bored, but when I arrived he would jump up and down. When Wynn became ill and was in hospital for three weeks, I looked after Robbie. She came home and I visited every day; we would talk about spirituality and she told me that she had lost her daughter only a few weeks before and in fact both her daughters had died young.

"Oh, someone has put their arms around me," she said suddenly one day. "It feels like angel wings squeezing me. And I know my husband is here because I can smell his Old Spice aftershave." I was able to give her a few personal messages from her husband and she said that nobody else had known what I told her. Later, I asked her what her plans were for Christmas. "Just me and Robbie and a potted meat sandwich," she said. Well, of course, I brought her to my house to have Christmas with the family and that made her happy.

In the New Year she said to me, "Can I ask you something? I've hung on until I found someone I could trust to look after my Robbie. Will you please look after him when I've gone?"

Wynn was becoming very breathless and I knew her time was up when I saw her daughter standing beside her; she looked at me and said, "I have come for me Mam." Wynn died soon afterwards and her solicitor told me that she had left Robbie as a gift to me in her Will. I took Robbie to her funeral along with a posy of flowers I'd made and as I stood by the graveside I heard her whisper, "Thank you, I love you both." A few weeks later I saw her again in my bedroom, looking down at Robbie and smiling.

Any psychic will tell you that it's really difficult to do readings or make predictions for your own family, and I've never done it. But my daughter Karen was single and living alone with Clyde, her adorable Japanese Akita dog who looked more like a giant panda. Karen worked long hours, sometimes having to be away from home for conferences, and Clyde was becoming very ill. The situation was getting her down badly and one day she asked me whether I thought there was 'anyone out there' for her.

Before I could even object that I couldn't do a reading for her, I was shown the man she would marry. Straight away I told her that, yes, she would meet him in the next few weeks, he was very different to her other boyfriends, he travels a lot and Spirit had given me the name 'Ray'.

"I shouldn't have asked," she said. "I know you can't read for family. 'Ray' is an old man's name." Not a vote of confidence from my daughter, then.

Two weeks later, she went out with friends and as she walked into the pub – one that I'd gone into fifty-four years earlier – she saw a gorgeous man. He must have thought the same about her because he came over, bought her a drink and they sat chatting until his friend came over and asked, "Who is this beautiful girl, Ray?" He had been travelling and had only come to our city for a night out. Karen phoned me later that evening to say she had met her soulmate; later, they got married and are very happy.

When I saw her in her wedding dress, coming through the door with her Dad, I saw in the background her Nan Flora (my husband's mother) wearing her favourite blue dress with white flowers. Karen said, "I wish Nan could have been here" so I told her that she was walking behind her. There are little orbs on the photos we took then.

Actually, we do seem to be keeping things in the family. When my daughter was training to be a hypnotherapist and was about to take her exams, she needed someone to practise on. Oh, why did I let myself be persuaded? She regressed me back to a past life where I seemed to be a Wise Woman or witch. I was in a smokey hut with a dog and a cat, there was an open fire burning and I could smell something earthy, perhaps herbs bubbling away in a big pot over the fire. I had long dark hair and wore a grey dress tied around the middle with string. Nearby there were other people like me in their huts.

Then I heard shouting, "Kill the witch!" I kept quiet but two men ran in and dragged me out by the hair, pulled me to the river and held me under the water until I drowned. (Even to this day I am petrified of water. After my accident at work, my husband paid for swimming lessons for me to help me get better but I still dared not get in the water.)

However, there was an interesting 'benefit' from my past life… For some occupational therapy, a friend gave me some Hallowe'en fabric and my husband bought me a sewing machine; I found some fabric faces in a charity shop and another friend bought me a book of unusual patterns for making dolls – and a book of spells! So I made a few small 'witch dolls', advertised them on social media and since then I have made hundreds of them. One lady asked me to make her a fertility witch because she had miscarried four times, so I decorated a doll with charms and a moonstone crystal and included a spell. She rang me ten months later to say she'd had a baby boy. Later I started offering Romany dolls along with a five-card psychic reading and they've gone all over the world, from Australia to America and Europe inbetween. Half of all the proceeds goes to kidney disease research and animal welfare.

Mediums sometimes have readings from other mediums! A friend of mine told me a while ago, "You are going to write a book." No way, I thought, I'm far too busy with my witch dolls, sending them all over the world, and my other work. But then I remembered all the stories of ghosts and spirits that I'd noted down over the years – perhaps I could put them into a book after all, to give people hope when they think the world is against them and to tell people that we are never alone, the angels and Spirit are nearby for us.

But which publisher would be the right one to help me? Thinking about this, I went into the animal rescue charity shop I support and two books published by Local Legend were on display...

If you have enjoyed this book...

Local Legend is committed to publishing the very best spiritual writing, both fiction and non-fiction. You might also enjoy:

POWER FOR GOOD
David J Serlin (ISBN 978-1-910027-31-8)

When we say "Yes!" to the subtle invitations of Spirit, we may find ourselves on exciting journeys of discovery and learning, drawing to ourselves a universal Power for Good that changes us forever. David describes how a chance encounter – and an open mind – led to almost incredible psychic experiences and revelations of spiritual teachings that took him and his wife Linda on a whole new path and new careers. He tells their story here and sets out, in down-to-earth language and with humour, the principles for a happy and fulfilled life.

DAY TRIPS TO HEAVEN
T J Hobbs (ISBN 978-1-907203-99-2)

The author's debut novel is a brilliant description of life in the spiritual worlds and of the guidance available to all of us on Earth as we struggle to be the best we can. Ethan is learning to be a spirit guide but having a hard time of it, with too many questions and too much self-doubt. But he has potential, so is given a special dispensation to bring a few deserving souls for a preview of the afterlife, to help them with crucial decisions they have to make in life on Earth. The book is full of gentle humour, compassion and spiritual knowledge, and it asks important questions of us all.

A UNIVERSAL GUIDE TO HAPPINESS
Joanne Gregory (ISBN 978-1-910027-06-6)

Joanne is an internationally acclaimed clairaudient medium with a celebrity contact list. Growing up, she ignored her evident psychic abilities, fearful of standing out from others, and even later, despite witnessing miracles daily, her life was difficult. But then she began to learn the difference between the psychic and the spiritual, and her life turned round.

This is her spiritual reference handbook – a guide to living happily and successfully in harmony with the energy that created our universe. It is the knowledge and wisdom distilled from a lifetime's experience of working with Spirit.

THE QUIRKY MEDIUM
Alison Wynne-Ryder (ISBN 978-1-907203-47-3)

Alison is the co-host of the TV show *Rescue Mediums*, in which she puts herself in real danger to free homes of lost and often malicious spirits. Yet she is a most reluctant medium, afraid of ghosts! This is her amazing and often very funny autobiography, taking us 'back stage' of the television production as well as describing how she came to discover the psychic gifts that have brought her an international following.

Winner of the Silver Medal in the national Wishing Shelf Book Awards.

SIMPLY SPIRITUAL
Jacqui Rogers (ISBN 978-1-907203-75-6)

The 'spookies' started contacting Jacqui when she was a child and never gave up until, at last, she developed her psychic talents and became the successful international medium she is now. This is a powerful and moving account of her difficult life and her triumph over adversity, with many great stories of her spiritual readings. The book was a Finalist in The People's Book Prize national awards.

AURA CHILD
A I Kaymen (ISBN 978-1-907203-71-8)

One of the most astonishing books ever written, telling the true story of a genuine Indigo child. Genevieve grew up in a normal London family but from an early age realised that she had very special spiritual and psychic gifts. She saw the energy fields around living things, read people's thoughts and even found herself slipping through time and able to converse with the spirits of those who had lived in her neighbourhood. This is an uplifting and inspiring book for what it tells us about the nature of our minds.

CELESTIAL AMBULANCE
Ann Matkins (ISBN 978-1-907203-45-9)

A brave and delightful comedy novel. Having died of cancer, Ben wakes up in the afterlife looking forward to a good rest, only to find that everyone is expected to get a job! He becomes the driver of an ambulance (with a mind of her own), rescuing the spirits of others who have died suddenly and delivering them safely home. This book is as thought-provoking as it is entertaining.

5P1R1T R3V3L4T10N5
Nigel Peace (ISBN 978-1-907203-14-5)

With descriptions of more than a hundred proven prophetic dreams and many more everyday synchronicities, the author shows us that, without doubt, we can know the future and that everyone can receive genuine spiritual guidance for our lives' challenges. World-renowned biologist Dr Rupert Sheldrake has endorsed this book as "...vivid and fascinating... pioneering research... " and it was national runner-up in The People's Book Prize awards.

TAP ONCE FOR YES

Jacquie Parton (ISBN 978-1-907203-62-6)

This extraordinary book offers powerful evidence of human survival after death. When Jacquie's son Andrew suddenly committed suicide, she was devastated. But she was determined to find out whether his spirit lived on, and began to receive incredible yet undeniable messages from him on her mobile phone... Several others also then described deliberate attempts at spirit contact. This is a story of astonishing love and courage, as Jacquie fought her own grief and others' doubts in order to prove to the world that her son still lives.

These titles are available as paperbacks and eBooks. Further details and extracts of these and many other beautiful books may be seen at

www.local-legend.co.uk

CPSIA information can be obtained
at www.ICGtesting.com
Printed in the USA
BVHW062355261221
624770BV00007B/513